HUMILITY OF HEART

From the Italian of

Fr CAJETAN MARY DA BERGAMO

Capuchin

By

HERBERT CARDINAL VAUGHAN

Martino Fine Books
Eastford, CT
2023

Publisher's Note

This Martino Fine Books edition is a facsimile of the 1944 edition published by the Newman Bookshop, Westminster, Maryland. The text of the Newman Press edition contains numbered sections, some of which are missing from the 1944 edition. These missing sections are likely the result either of typographical error or perhaps they represent sections from the original Italian edition purposely omitted by Cardinal Vaughan in his translation. Whatever the case, we thought it appropriate to mention this anomaly from the original 1944 edition, which is carried over into our edition.

Martino Fine Books
P.O. Box 913,
Eastford, CT 06242 USA

ISBN   978-1-68422-798-3

Copyright 2023

Martino Fine Books

Cover Design Tiziana Matarazzo

Printed in the United States of America On 100% Acid-Free Paper

HUMILITY OF HEART

From the Italian of
Fr CAJETAN MARY DA BERGAMO
Capuchin

By
HERBERT CARDINAL VAUGHAN

THE NEWMAN BOOKSHOP
WESTMINSTER, MARYLAND
1944

THE NEWMAN BOOKSHOP
WESTMINSTER, MD.

19944

To
The priests ordained by me
For the Diocese of Salford
And the Archdiocese of Westminster
And for the
foreign missions.

Also to
The Ladies of Charity
Established by me in
Salford and Westminster,

In the conviction that
Their works of charity, if planted in
The garden of humility,
Will bear a fuller and
Richer harvest than if sown in
Any other soil.

Herbert Cardinal Vaughan
Archbishop of Westminster
April 23, 1903

Publisher's Preface

HUMILITY OF HEART is one of the few books on the virtue of humility, and it is probably the best! As the author points out in several places, humility is typical of all Saints; it is the underlying virtue of all virtues; and as the author shows, the easiest way to acquire all other virtues is to concentrate first on acquiring humility.

What exactly is humility? It is definitely *not* a grovelling self-deprecation or even low self-esteem. Rather, it is an accurate view of oneself and where one stands in relation to all others, but especially where one stands in relationship to God and how difficult it is for a person consistently to perform supernaturally good acts purely from a motive of love of God.

Humility, as the author points out, is diametrically opposed to the Capital Sin of Pride and wars against that powerful inclination within fallen man. Before we can commit any sin, we have to commit the sin of Pride, for as Scripture says, *"Pride goeth before the destruction, and the spirit is lifted up before a fall."* (*Proverbs* 16:18). Also, before every sin we commit, we have to lie to ourselves that it is *not* a sin, or at least that our sin

vii

is *not so bad* as we may think. Thus, lying blots
out humility because it purposely obscures the
truth and is directly opposed to the virtue of
humility, which sees the exact truth of things.

Now Pride can take on many and very subtle
forms, deceiving even the most intelligent of spiritual aspirants. It is the one Capital Sin that even
the highly principled and noble-minded can fall
into. Often, as Father da Bergamo points out, it is
the one sin that ensnares the intelligent, edu-
cated, highly moral person, even him who is dedicated to God's work. Whereas such highly
disciplined and enlightened people would perhaps
never descend to Gluttony, Lust, Covetousness,
Avarice, etc., they nonetheless will often succumb
to some subtle form of Pride.

The author repeatedly says here that *if one
thinks he is humble, he is not!* This is a very dis-
couraging thought! And the reader should be prepared *not* to become discouraged by what he or
she will encounter in this seemingly simple little
book. For *Humility of Heart* tackles the greatest
spiritual enemy man has, his own pride, which
per Sacred Scripture itself, (*Proverbs* 16:18)—
along with lying—precedes every sin. Now we
know that everyone commits some sins. As the
Bible says, "For a just man shall fall seven times
and shall rise again." (*Proverbs* 24:16). Therefore,
everyone is proud—to some extent at least. The
logic is inescapable. And therefore, *Humility of
Heart* is addressing mankind's biggest problem:
pride-filled lying, which precedes every sin that

all human beings engage in—at least to some slight degree—despite what might be their great education, learning, accomplishments, status, honor, esteem, rank, adulation, etc.

Thus, acquiring true humility and also properly assessing the enormity of the job one shoulders in honestly pursuing humility is nothing short of the toughest assignment one will ever undertake. But we *must* undertake it, for Our Lord has admonished us: *"Learn of me, for I am meek and humble of heart." (Matthew* 11:29). The neophyte to serious spirituality, therefore, should be on his guard against discouragement at the prospect of attaining this essential virtue. It will entail a spiritual sort of "hand-to-hand combat" that will continue all one's life and battle him right to the end. For it is a struggle against the most profound, inherent flaw in human nature—Pride.

Once overcome, however, all the other virtues follow in its train rather easily. The beginner in the spiritual life simply has to be aware of the strength of this powerful adversary he is challenging in attempting to acquire humility—it is his very own corrupt, often miserable self, his own nature at its deepest, most selfish level, inherited through Original Sin from our first parents, Adam and Eve!

Attaining humility, therefore, is *the great battle* in life, the one that will lead (through success) to sanctity and salvation, but (through defeat) to sin and perdition. It is a light, little book you hold,

Dear Reader, but one outlining the greatest fight you will ever enter—the battle to overcome your own prideful self, as you war against "the world, the flesh and the devil." But the stakes are high, and the results eternal, one way or the other.

Cardinal Vaughan's brother indicates that the Cardinal carried an Italian copy of this book with him, to read from again and again. It would behoove us all to read it at least *several* times—periodically—to impress its truths firmly upon our minds.

In passing, one cannot help admiring the Cardinal's intrepidity in translating this essential book during the last days of his life, when he must have known he was dying. He could have easily and without criticism simply engaged his final days in a long retreat and self-examination before meeting Our Lord, but besides doing something like that, he also labored to bequeath this spiritual gem to the English-speaking world and thus ultimately to make it available everywhere. May God reward him for doing so and may you the reader be rewarded for taking up its challenge.

—Thomas A Nelson
Original Publisher
February 7, 2006
St. Romuald–Abbot
St. Richard of Lucca–King

Original Preface

THESE "Thoughts and Sentiments on Humility" were written by Cardinal Vaughan during the last months of his life. Being ordered out of London by his medical advisers, the Cardinal went to Derwent, where, as the guest of Lord and Lady Edmund Talbot, he found that perfect freedom and multitude of peace of which he had long felt the need.

It was while reposing his soul in quiet prayer and feasting his sight on the fine scenery of this ideal spot among the moorlands of Derbyshire, that the thought came to him of translating, while yet there was time, Father Cajetan's treatise on humility.

For more than thirty years Cardinal Vaughan had known and studied that work, and it is scarcely an exaggeration to say that he had made it during the last fourteen years of his life his constant companion, his *vade mecum*—[literally, "go with me"; a handy reference book one carries].

What lessons it had taught him, what sights it had shown him, what stories it had told him, those only know to whom he revealed his inmost soul. However even those who knew the Cardinal less intimately could scarcely fail to realize in their dealings with him that they were treating with a man whose growing characteristic was humility of heart. A more truly humble man I have seldom if ever come across. It was the humility of a child; it was so sweet and simple, and yet so strong and saint-like—may I not even venture to say, Christ-like?

It was the sort of humility that could not go wrong, for it was founded on truth. It *was* truth! Does not St. Bernard remind us that "Humility is truth?" It is a truth which, inasmuch as it is a home-thrusting truth, none of us can afford to ignore. It is the truth all about oneself in one's triple alliance with God, with one's neighbor, with one's own soul.

Humility may not inappropriately be called the starting post in that race for Heaven of which the Apostle speaks. It is the *terminus a quo*—"the end to which" one ultimately tends—in the spiritual life. It is the first of the many lessons set before us in the school of sanctity—a difficult lesson, I grant you, and one which Nature seeks to shirk or to put off indefinitely, but for the man who means to graduate to Heaven, there is no escape from it. Accordingly, our Divine Master . . . reminds all His would-be followers, without distinction, that they must learn this lesson, get it well by heart, and into the heart; for Humility is the alphabet out of which every other virtue is formed and built up. It is the soil of the garden of the soul, "the good ground" on which the Divine Sower goes forth to sow His seed.

It is in the school of Christ and from the lips of Christ Himself that we must learn humility. "Learn of Me, because I am meek and humble of heart." (*Matt.* 11:29). By following the Master Himself, by studying His own Heart, we have to acquire, to appreciate and to practice this first, this vital, this vitalizing, energizing virtue—without which no man can hope to make any progress at all on the Royal Road heavenward.

So all-important for us creatures is the acquisition of humility that Our Divine Lord became man in order to put before us in His Own Person this great object-lesson in its most attractive beauty. "He humbled Himself." "He emptied Himself." He became the humblest of the humble because, as St. Augustine points out, the "Divine Master was unwilling to teach what He Himself was not; He was unwilling to command what He Himself did not practice."

With Our Dear and Blessed Lord as our great example of humility, we may well—one and all of us—set about practicing, with some hope of success, this indispensable virtue, this *maximum bonum*—"greatest good"—as St. Thomas calls it.

To his own soul Cardinal Vaughan found so much benefit from the cultivation in it of humility, that he resolved, at no small cost to himself, in the feeble state in which he then was, to gird himself and to go forth sowing broadcast into the soil of the hearts of the laity, as well as of the clergy, this despised little mustard seed of which men speak so much but know so little.

It was Padre Gaetano's work on humility that had been the instrument in God's hand of helping the Cardinal. Accordingly, in his zeal for souls, he proposed to put it into English, in order to bring the work within the reach of all who care for the health, growth and strength of their own individual souls in solid virtue.

That the Cardinal has left us a precious legacy in this treatise on humility will, I feel sure, be the verdict of all who study or who only peruse these pages, rendered into English from the Italian of the devout Minor Capuchin, whose death occurred two centuries ago [d. 1753].

Between the covers of this unpretending volume there is nourishment for all who "hunger and thirst after justice" (*Matt.* 5:6). For the proficient in the spiritual life, as well as for the beginner, humility, as it were, is holding in itself all those elements that are needed to build up the strong Christian man. In humility, the soul will find a sovereign remedy for its many ills, a matchless balm for its many wounds, while a soul-beauty all its own will spring up in all who shall learn how to use it wisely, under the guidance of the Holy Spirit. "He who is truly humble," says St. Bernard, "knows how to convert all his humiliations into humility," while out of humility, God can raise a soul to what otherwise might be giddy heights of sanctity. If anyone should need a proof of this statement, I will refer him to any chapter in the life of any Saint in our Calendar. For a moment, gaze into the face of "the Woman clothed with the Sun" (*Apoc.* 12:1), and remember the words, "*Respexit humilitatem ancillæ suæ*"—"He hath regarded the humility of his handmaid." (*Luke* 1:48). The height of Mary's sanctity is gauged by the depth of her humility: "*Exaltavit humiles*"—"He shall exalt the humble."

To the Clergy and Ladies of Charity, to whom the Cardinal dedicates these "Thoughts and Sentiments," this volume will come with very special meaning. It enshrines the last words of a great churchman, of a truly spiritual man, while it conveys a special message from the Cardinal's heart to all readers.

This treatise is a sort of last will and testament of Cardinal Vaughan, bequeathed to those with whom he was most intimately associated in work for the good of souls. It is a legacy from one who made humility a life-long study and who had more opportunities than most of us know of making tremendous strides in it, through the humiliations which he welcomed as most precious opportunities offered him by God for the salvation and sanctification of his soul. May he rest in peace.

Bernard Vaughan, S.J.
Derwent Hall,
August 8, 1905.

Introduction

FATHER Cajetan, or Padre Gaetano Maria da Bergamo, was one of the great Italian missionaries of the eighteenth century. Born in 1672, he was professed a Minor Capuchin in 1692, and died in 1753. His eulogy, contained in the work on Illustrious Writers of the Order of Minor Capuchins, is brief and pregnant: *"In religiosae vitae moribus nemini secundus, in omni genere scribendi facile primus."* ["Second to none in the customs of religious life, first in writing with ease on things of every kind."]

He was one of the reformers of the Italian pulpit, substituting for the vapid, empty rhetoric which then prevailed, a solid, learned and instructive style, animated by zeal and real devotion.

His religious works, written amid missions and courses of sermons, are contained in thirty volumes; of his writings Benedict XIV says that "they have this rare quality in our day, that they satisfy the intellect and the heart; their solid doctrine in no way dries up their tender devotion, and their devotional sweetness in no way detracts from the perfect solidity of their doctrine." He was a model religious, remarkable for his charity, zeal and love for God and for souls, which he had built up in the solid foundation of profound humility, with which he united a tender devotion to the Blessed Virgin.

I confess that, though I have been in possession of the Monza edition of his work for over thirty years, it was not till recently that I looked seriously into them. The first of his volumes is the one that has most struck me; and this I took up thirteen or fourteen years ago and have never put it down since. For it seems to supply so much of what the soul most needs, and which everyone must feel that he can never possess sufficiently, if even he possess it really at all, namely *Humility of Heart*.

There is a great advantage in using such a book as this for two or three years consecutively as a meditation book. The human mind is so volatile, the character so restless, convictions are so slow in taking a deep and permanent hold on our practical life, that I have always considered that a retreat made upon one idea, and two or three years given to the meditation on one great subject is productive of more solid good than the following out of the ordinary system, which of course has its own advantages, commending it to the greater number. I venture even to think that for many persons living amidst the distractions of the world, such as priests engaged in the active ministry and devout men and women of the laity who are deeply in earnest about the work of their sanctification, the persevering study of one book for years—such as the *Spiritual Combat*, St.

Alphonsus on *Prayer*, Blessed [now "Saint" Louis] De Montfort on *True Devotion to the Blessed Virgin Mary*, Padre Gaetano on *Humility of Heart*, Palma on *The Passion*, and certain other treatises which need not be named here—is far more important than for recluses and good people living out of the world. We never get a proper hold of a great spiritual doctrine until we have lived in it and been saturated by it. The soul must soak in the brine until it has become wholly impregnated with its qualities. And is this process likely to be carried out by one who thirsts for variety and is always on the move towards some totally new sensation from the one that at present occupies his feelings? There is the question of breadth, I know, as well as depth. But he who said *"Times hominem unius libri"* ["Fear the man of one book"] hit a truth that must be felt by every earnest soul.

One need not fear that the constant handling of one book will dry up the mind, if the topic treated be one of primary importance and if it be the work of a master on the spiritual life. The number of thoughts and truths suggested by such a book are truly wonderful. It often will happen that far more is suggested than is actually put down by the hand of the writer. But to enjoy this result, you must have put away all hurry; you must have said, "I am going to spend at least a year with this friend; I am going to take him, not merely for a friend, but for a master and a guide." I well remember how one night before bedtime, reading my da Bergamo in the Chapel of St. Bede's College, a single line suggested this idea or train of thought, God in the Old and New Testaments, named people after their personal characteristics. Now, were I to name myself after my personal traits, I might name myself by the names of the Seven Capital Sins. These are the innate springs of evil within me. They are the heads and sources from which all other sins take their rise. They are like the gall spots, the sour or iron oozings that often disfigure a whole field that has been neither drained nor cultivated. Indeed they are much more mischievous and fatal than these, for they are capable of overflowing and destroying everything that is good and profitable.

The springs of these evil tendencies are so deeply imbedded in our nature that is is almost impossible to get rid of them altogether. The doing so is the work of a lifetime, unless we be able to get below the main well-spring of them all, and so inflict a permanent injury on them all. I may, therefore, take myself in hand thus, and say: "In the name of God, I will call you what you really are, *Pride, Covetousness, Lust, Anger, Gluttony, Envy, Sloth;* and I will add to these Seven Capital Sins five other characteristics of my soul, viz., *Weakness, Ignorance, Poverty, Theft* and *Cruelty*—twelve names which may not be the less appropriate because I do not desire to be publicly known by them: twelve names that may bring home to me some truths and which may be exceedingly good and valuable for private use. For the first thing is to begin by a profound knowledge of oneself, and of one's own miseries—though it may not be wise or prudent to begin by proclaiming one's sins to the world. Some of these names may be obviously applicable to ourselves, such as Weakness, Ignorance and Poverty. For how weak and ignorant we are, physically and morally! How dependent upon others for the things of commonest use! How poor, too, in grace and virtue and every kind of excellence, especially if compared with many others.

The title of Theft is not so very obvious until we recognize that instead of giving glory to God for every good thing we may seem to do or to possess, we rob Him of this glory as much as we can, in the most natural and thoughtless manner, and attribute to ourselves and appropriate from others to ourselves all the credit and glory of any little thing we do. He who makes this his habit may very deservedly be named a *thief* or "Theft," calling himself by the act he is habitually doing and is habitually famous for. But *Cruelty*, how is this name justified? I have never been fond of giving pain to animals, at least not since I was a senseless child: why should I be called "Cruelty"? We have only to remember and understand that—by our sins we crucify again to ourselves the Son of God—to realize how well deserving we are of the name of *Cruelty*. We give wanton pain to an animal, and we are punished by the law; we are cruel to children, and we are prosecuted; we inflict pain unnecessarily on our friends and dependents, and we are justly esteemed heartless brutes. It is only Our Lord Jesus Christ, only Our Lord God and Father in Heaven whom we may treat with wanton injury and insult, disobedience and neglect, and escape without any name or mark of contempt and disapproval. I have but to consider my own share in the sorrows and Passion and Death of Jesus Christ, and how His Mother participated in all He suffered, to see how truly I have been a monster of *Cruelty.* And so it seems that in this simple way, by merely repeating thoughtfully these our twelve vicious names to ourselves, we may become each time a little better grounded in the truth inculcated by this admirable treatise on "Humility of Heart."

All this to some may seem fanciful, and they may brush it away as unworthy of consideration. But to others it will not be so, especially if they are given "to ponder over these things in their hearts." [Cf. *Luke* 2:19: "But Mary kept all these words, pondering *them* in her heart."] Such thoughts may be particularly serviceable at certain times. For instance, if you are receiving public homage and addresses in circumstances of unusual pomp and ceremony; or if you happen to be, from your position, the object of any other special veneration, and certain noxious fumes of vanity or self-complacency be found ascending for a moment to your head, an obvious remedy is to reflect that it is not yourself, but your office that is receiving such special honor, and that anyone else occupying the same position would be the object of just the same respect. But better still than this will it be quietly to call yourself over [again] by the twelve names drawn from your moral qualities and tendencies. The noxious gas is then extinguished; the decked-out worm that you are is crushed in its own exuding slime beneath your feet; and you realize at once that you are playing a part which receives honor due to your official, not to your private, character.

Of course, it is only a small number who are in a position to receive public honors and addresses. But there is no one who is not the recipient from time to time of praise and admiration; and when this seems stinted in kind or quantity, our pride and self-love quickly rises up to supply the defect. It is on these occasions that the slow and measured recital to yourself of our twelve names will scatter the fumes of vanity and leave you in the full enjoyment of a multitude of peace.

But above all, we priests have to bear in mind that, as true representatives of Jesus Christ, we must wear His livery and become truly meek and humble of heart. Without this, He will not know us, except "afar off"—*et alta a longe cognoscit* ["and the high he knoweth afar off." *Psalm* 137:6]. This humility must be consistent and of universal application. We must be humble with our fellow-priests and humble with those with whom we work. The priest is likened by Christ to a fisherman—a fisherman working with his nets, mending them, caring for them, using them to catch fish. He is not represented as fishing with a worm or as throwing the fly, but as working with his net. The net used by us priests is a rational net, made up of good people who co-operate with us. Thus, Our Lord Himself used the Apostles and disciples and women, as well as preaching with His own mouth. The Apostles did the same. Read the closing sentences to several of the Pauline Epistles to see how many lay people, men and women, rich and poor, He used as forming part of His net to catch souls.

There is a great need in the present day to make use of the Catholic laity in the salvation of souls. The priest must use them like a net held in his hand; he must care for his net, not be surprised if its meshes break from time to time and if they need to be mended.

The rock on which the Ladies of Charity and other lay people who are zealous to help the clergy in apostolic work for souls so often founder is one or other of the many forms of pride. They are unwilling to be guided, to be contradicted, to be restrained in their ardor. They see and above all *feel* things so clearly, so keenly, that they cannot imagine that they are going too fast, doing too much and perhaps spoiling other good work done by persons who deserve consideration. They fully realize that they are impelled by zeal and enthusiasm and that no one just now comes up to them, but they do not know and realize how unsteady and fickle they really are and that it will require only a very moderate amount of coldness or contradiction to throw them off the line and to discourage and fill them with such feelings of annoyance and indifference as will lead them to throw up everything in disgust. Thus they end by doing more harm than they have done good. And all this because they are wanting in the first principles of humility. I should like every Lady of Charity to study this book well, to make it the foundation of her practical life. The result would be that she would become secretly a saint before God, and that she would in the course of her life do ten times, a hundred times, more than she could ever accomplish without humility, *"Humilia respicit in terra, et alta a longe cognoscit,"* says the Psalmist, when speaking of God's dealings with men. ["For the Lord is high, and looketh on the low: and the high he knoweth afar off."—*Psalm* 137:6].

Like all good works, the conversion and salvation of souls are really the work of the Holy Ghost. He employs means and instruments. Happy are we if He employ us, if He associate us in this way with Himself. Do you desire to persuade Him to use you? Do you long to attract Him? Well, there is no surer way than by the practice of humility. You must be humble toward God, toward His visible representatives (for thus you prove your humility toward God), toward your fellow workers, and toward the people whom you must serve lovingly, humbly, patiently, as though you were dealing with Christ.

I have the strongest possible conviction that Our Lord desires to be served, especially in a country like England, where we are "the little flock," by a great development of religious activity among the laity, acting in co-operation with and under the guidance of the clergy. But I am equally convinced that unless these new workers are formed on the humility of heart which Our Lord told all of us to learn of Him, they and their overtures will be rejected by God and man. It is for this reason that I have dedicated this volume, written by a most holy and learned missionary, many times commended by zealous popes and bishops, to the Ladies of Charity, as well as to the priests for whose ordination I have been responsible.

—Herbert Cardinal Vaughan
(1832-1903)

Contents

∾1∾

Thoughts and Sentiments on Humility

IN Paradise there are many Saints who never gave alms on earth: their poverty justified them. There are many Saints who never mortified their bodies by fasting or wearing hair shirts: their bodily infirmities excused them. There are many Saints too who were not virgins: their vocation was otherwise. But in Paradise there is no Saint who was not humble.

God banished Angels from Heaven for their pride; therefore, how can we pretend to enter therein if we do not keep ourselves in a state of humility? Without humility, says St. Peter Damian (*Serm.* 45), not even the Virgin Mary herself, with her incomparable virginity, could have entered into the glory of Christ, and we ought to be convinced of this truth that, though destitute of some of the other virtues, we may yet be saved, but never without humility. There are people who flatter themselves that they have done much by preserving unsullied chastity, and truly chastity is a beautiful adornment; but as the angelic St. Thomas says: "Speaking

1

absolutely, humility excels virginity."[1]

We often study diligently to guard against and correct ourselves of the vices of concupiscence, which belong to a sensual and animal nature, and this inward conflict which the body wages *adversus carnem*—"against the flesh"—(*Gal.* 5:17) is truly a spectacle worthy of God and of His angels. But, alas, how rarely do we use this diligence and caution to conquer spiritual vices, of which pride is the first and the greatest of all, and which sufficed of itself to transform an angel into a demon!

2. Jesus Christ calls us all into His school to learn, not to work miracles, nor to astonish the world by marvellous enterprises, but to be humble of heart. "Learn of Me, because I am meek and humble of heart." (*Matt.* 11:29). He has not called everyone to be doctors, preachers or priests, nor has He bestowed on all the gift of restoring sight to the blind, healing the sick, raising the dead or casting out devils, but to all He has said: "Learn of Me, to be humble of heart," and to all He has given the power to learn humility of Him. Innumerable things are worthy of imitation in the Incarnate Son of God, but He only asks us to imitate His humility. What then? Must we suppose that all the treasures of Divine Wisdom which were in Christ are to be reduced to the virtue of humility? "So it certainly is,"[2] answers

---

1. *Simpliciter loquendo humilitas virginitatem excedit.* (4 dist., Q. 33, art. 3 ad 6; et 22, Q. 161, art. 5.)
2. *Ita plane.* (*Lib. de sancta virginit.*, c. 35.)

St. Augustine. Humility contains all things because in this virtue is truth; therefore, God must also dwell therein, since He is the Truth.

The Saviour might have said: "Learn of Me to be chaste, humble, prudent, just, wise, abstemious, etc." But He only says: "Learn of Me, because I am meek and humble of heart." (*Matt.* 11:29). And in humility alone He includes all things, because as St. Thomas so truly says, "Acquired humility is in a certain sense the greatest good."[3] Therefore whoever possesses this virtue may be said, as to his proximate disposition, to possess all virtues, and he who lacks it, lacks all.

3. Reading the works of St. Augustine, we find in them all that his sole idea was the exaltation of God above the creature as far as possible, and as far as possible, the humble subjection of the creature to God. The recognition of this truth should find a place in every Christian mind, thus establishing—according to the acuteness and penetration of our intelligence—a sublime conception of God and a lowly and vile conception of the creature. But we can only succeed in doing this by humility.

Humility is in reality a confession of the greatness of God, who after His voluntary self-annihilation, was exalted and glorified; wherefore, Holy

---

3. *Humilitas acquisita est maximum bonum secundum quid.* (*Lib. de Verit.*, Q. 1, art. 1. ad 3: et art. 19 ad 7).

Writ says: "For great is the power of God alone, and He is honored by the humble." (*Ecclus.* 3:21).

It was for this reason that God pledged Himself to exalt the humble and continually showers new graces upon them in return for the glory He constantly receives from them. Hence the Inspired Word again reminds us: "The greater thou art, the more humble thyself in all things, and thou shalt find grace before God." (*Ecclus.* 3:20).

The humblest man honors God most by his humility, and has the reward of being more glorified by God, who has said: "Whosoever shall glorify me, him will I glorify." (*1 Kings* 2:30). Oh, if we could only see how great is the glory of the humble in Heaven!

4. Humility is a virtue that belongs essentially to Christ, not only as man, but more especially as God, because with God, to be good, holy and merciful is not virtue, but nature; and humility is only a virtue. God cannot exalt Himself above what He is in His most high Being, nor can He increase His vast and infinite greatness; but He can humble Himself, as in fact He did humble and lower Himself. "He humbled Himself, He emptied Himself" (*Phil.* 2:7, 8), revealing Himself to us, through His humility, as the Lord of all virtues, the conqueror of the world, of death, of Hell and of sin.

No greater example of humility can be given than that of the Only Son of God when "the Word was made Flesh." Nothing could be more sublime than the words of St. John's Gospel, "In the beginning was the Word." And no abasement can be deeper than that which follows: "And the Word was made Flesh." By this union of the Creator with the creature, the Highest was united with the lowest. Jesus Christ summed up all His heavenly doctrine in humility, and before teaching it, it was His Will to practice it perfectly Himself. As St. Augustine says: "He was unwilling to teach what He Himself was not, He was unwilling to command what He Himself did not practice."[4]

But to what purpose did He do all this, if not that by this means all His followers should learn humility by practical example? He is our Master, and we are His disciples; but what profit do we derive from His teachings, which are practical and not theoretical?

How shameful it would be for anyone, after studying for many years in a school of art or science, under the teaching of excellent masters, if he were still to remain absolutely ignorant! My shame is great indeed, because I have lived so many years in the school of Jesus Christ, and yet I have learned nothing of that holy humility which He sought so earnestly to teach me. "Have mercy upon me according to Thy Word. Thou art good, and in Thy goodness teach me Thy justifications. Give me understanding, and I will learn Thy commandments." (*Ps.* 118:58, 68, 73).

———————

4. "*Noluit docere quod ipse non esset, noluit jubere quod ipse non faceret.*" (*Lib. de Sanct. Virginit.*, c. 36).

5. There is a kind of humility which is of counsel and of perfection, such as that which desires and seeks the contempt of others; but there is also a humility which is of necessity and of precept, without which, says Christ, we cannot enter into the kingdom of Heaven: "You shall not enter into the kingdom of Heaven." (*Matt.* 18:3). And this consists in not esteeming ourselves and in not wishing to be esteemed by others above what we really are.

No one can deny this truth, that humility is essential to all those who wish to be saved. "No one reaches the kingdom of Heaven except by humility," says St. Augustine.[5]

But practically speaking, I ask, what is this humility which is so necessary? When we are told that faith and hope are necessary, it is also explained to us in what we are to believe and to hope. In like manner, when humility is said to be necessary, in what should its practice consist, except in the lowest opinion of ourselves? It is in this moral sense that the humility of the heart has been explained by the Fathers of the Church. But can I say with truth that I possess this humility, which I recognize as necessary and obligatory? What care or solicitude do I display to acquire it? When a virtue is of precept [i.e., commanded], so is its practice also, as St. Thomas teaches. And therefore, as there is a humility

---

5. *"Ad regnum cœlorum nemo venit nisi per humilitatem sine aliis."* (*Lib. de Salut.* c. 32).

which is of precept, "it has its rule in the mind, viz., that one is not to esteem himself to be above that which he really is."[6]

How and when do I practice its acts, acknowledging and confessing my unworthiness before God? The following was the frequent prayer of St. Augustine, *Noscam Te, noscam me*—"May I know Thee; may I know myself!" And by this prayer he asked for humility, which is nothing else but a true knowledge of God and of oneself. To confess that God is what He is, the Omnipotent, "Great is the Lord, and exceedingly to be praised" (*Ps.* 47:1), and to declare that we are but nothingness before Him: "My substance is as nothing before Thee." (*Ps.* 38:6)—this is to be humble.

6. There is no valid excuse for not being humble, because we have always, within and without, abundant reasons for humility: "And thy humiliation shall be in the midst of thee." It is the Holy Ghost who sends us this warning by the mouth of His prophet Micheas. (*Micheas* 6:14).

When we consider well what we are in body and what we are in soul, it seems to me most easy to humble oneself and even most difficult to be proud. To be humble, it suffices that I should nourish within myself that right feeling—which belongs to every man who is honorable in the eyes of the world—to be content with one's own, with-

---

6. "*Et regulam habet in cognitione, ut scilicet aliquis non se existimet supra id esse quod est.*" (22, Q. 16, 2, art. 6).

out unjustly depriving our neighbor of what is his. Therefore, as I have nothing of my own but my own nothingness, it is sufficient for humility that I should be content with this nothingness. But if I am proud, I become like a thief, appropriating to myself that which is not mine, but God's. And most assuredly, it is a greater sin to rob God of that which belongs to God than to rob man of that which is man's.

To be humble, let us listen to the revelation of the Holy Ghost, which is infallible. "Behold you are of nothing, and your work of that which hath no being." (*Is.* 41:24). But who is really convinced of his own nothingness?

It is for this reason that in Holy Scripture it is said: "Every man is a liar." (*Ps.* 115:2). For there is no man who from time to time does not entertain some incredible self-esteem and form some false opinion as to his being, or having, or achieving something more than is possible to his own nothingness.

To know what our body is in reality, it will suffice for us to look into the grave, for from what we see there, we must inevitably conclude that, as it is with those decayed bodies, so it will soon be with us. And with this reflection, I must say to myself: "Why is earth and ashes proud?" (*Ecclus.* 10:9). Behold the glory of man! "For his glory is dung and worms; today he is lifted up, and tomorrow he shall not be found, because he is returned into his earth; and his thought is come to nothing." (*1 Mach.* 2:62, 63).

O my Soul, without going further to seek truth, enter in thought into the heart of thy dwelling, which is thy body! "Go in and shut thyself up in the midst of thy house." (*Ezech.* 3:24). Go in and look around thee well, and thou shalt find nothing but corruption. "Go into the clay and tread." (*Nahum* 3:14). Wherever thou turnest, thou wilt see nothing but putrefaction oozing forth.

In order to learn what we really are, let us examine our own conscience. And finding therein only our own malice and a capacity to commit every kind of iniquity, shall we not all say to ourselves: "Why dost thou glory in malice, thou that art mighty in iniquity?" (*Ps.* 51:1). What hast thou of thine own, My Soul, wherewith to glorify thyself—thou who art a vessel of iniquity and a sink of sin and vice? Is not all this self-glorification but vanity and deceit—whether it be for thy bodily or spiritual gifts that thou buildest a reputation for thyself?

Oh, how true it is that *every man is a liar,* for one need have but little pride in order to be a liar, and there is no one who has not inherited through our first parents something of that pride which they learned in listening to the deceitful promise of the serpent: "And you shall be as Gods." (*Gen.* 3:5).

Again it may be said that every man is a liar in this sense—that he not infrequently prizes earth more than Heaven, the body more than the soul, things temporal more than things eternal, the creature more than the Creator—and it is for this reason that David exclaims: "O ye sons of men, why do you love vanity and seek after lying?" (*Ps.* 4:3). "The sons of men are liars in the balances." (*Ps.* 61:10).

But in reality a lie dwells essentially in that pride which makes us esteem ourselves above what we are. Whoever regards himself as more than mere nothingness is filled with pride and is a liar. It is St. Paul's statement: "If any man think himself to be something, whereas he is nothing, he deceiveth himself." (*Gal.* 6:3).

Every time I esteem myself, preferring myself to others, I deceive myself with this self-adulation and commit an error against truth.

8. It is enough for a virgin to have fallen once for her to lose her virginity and for a wife to have been but once unfaithful for her to be perpetually dishonored; even though she may afterwards perform many noble works, still her dishonor can never be effaced, and the sting and painful memory of her shame and guilt must remain forever in her conscience.

And thus, even though in the whole course of my life I have only committed one sin, the fact will always remain that I have sinned and committed the worst and most ignominious action. And even if I should live a life of continual penance and be certain of God's forgiveness, and though the sin exist no longer in my conscience, still I shall always have cause for shame and humiliation in the fact that I have sinned: "My sin is always before me. To thee only have I sinned, and have done evil before thee." (*Ps.* 50:5, 6).

9. What should we say if we saw the public executioner walking in the streets and claiming to be esteemed, respected and honored? We should consider his effrontery as insufferable as his calling is infamous. And thou, my Soul, each time that thou hast sinned mortally, thou hast indeed been as an executioner, nailing to the Cross the Son of God! Thus St. Paul describes sinners as "crucifying again to themselves the Son of God." (*Heb.* 6:6).

And with this character of infamy, which thou bearest within thee, dost thou still dare to demand honor and esteem? Wilt thou still have the courage to say: "I insist upon being honored and respected, I will not be slighted?" However much pride may tempt me to boast and seek esteem, I have ample cause to blush with shame when I hear the voice of conscience reproaching me for my ignominy and my sins, and not ceasing to reprove me for being a perfidious and ungrateful rebel against God, a traitor and an executioner who co-operated in the Passion and Death of Jesus Christ. "All the day long my shame is before me: and the confusion of my face hath covered me at the voice of him that reproacheth me." (*Ps.* 43:16, 17).

10. We must acknowledge that one of the five reasons why we do not live in this necessary humility is that we do not fear the justice of God.

Look at a criminal, how humbly he stands before the judge, with lowered eyes, pallid face and bowed head: he knows that he has been convicted of atrocious crimes; he knows that thereby he has merited capital punishment and may justly be condemned to the gallows; and hence he fears, and his fear keeps him humble, chasing from his brain all thoughts of ambition and vainglory. So also the soul, conscious of the numerous sins it has committed, aware that it has indeed deserved Hell, and that from one moment to another it may be condemned to Hell by Divine Justice, fears the wrath of God; and this fear causes the soul to remain humble before Him; and if it does not feel this humility, it can only be because the fear of God is wanting: "There is no fear of God before his eyes." (*Ps.* 35:1). Oh, cry to God from your heart: "Pierce Thou my flesh with Thy fear." (*Ps.* 118:120).

And this holy fear, which is the beginning of wisdom, will also be the beginning of true humility; for as the Inspired Word says, humility and wisdom are inseparable companions: "Where humility is, there also is wisdom." (*Prov.* 11:2).

11. There is no Saint, however holy and innocent, who may not truly consider himself the greatest sinner in the world. It is enough that he knows himself to be man, to recognize that he is liable to commit all the evil of which man is capable. As man, I have in my corrupt nature a proclivity to every evil; and so far as I am concerned, I am quite capable of committing all kinds of sin; and if I do not commit them, it is through a special grace of God, which preserves and restrains me.

A tree does not fall while bending under its own weight, and this must be attributed to the strength of its support; and in the same way, if I have not fallen into every kind of iniquity, it must not be attributed to my own inherent virtue, but only to divine grace, which by its goodness has supported me. Therefore, how can I esteem myself more than another while we are all equal in human weakness? "For what is my strength?" (*Job* 6:11). I am a son of Adam, like every other man, born in sin, inclined to sin, and ever ready to fall into sin. I have no need of the devil to tempt me to sin; my own concupiscence is only too great a temptation; and if God were to withdraw from me His protecting and helping hand, I know that I should be precipitated headlong from bad to worse. When St. Augustine made his examen of conscience, he did not always find sufficient to excite within him sorrow and contrition, so he dwelt on those sins which he might or would have committed had he not been preserved from them by God's infinite mercy; and he grieved and accused himself and humbly implored pardon of God for the evil capacity he had to commit all kinds of heinous and impious sins. In this practice is to be found an exercise of true humility.

12. It has often happened that those who were more perfect than others have shamefully fallen, and this after a long period of good and virtuous works, showing the marvellous things that a man can do when helped by God's special grace, and who by their terrible fall have also testified to the iniquities of which a man is capable, if abandoned to himself and left to the weakness of his own free will.

God has shown His creative omnipotence by forming me out of nothing and making me a human being. Were God to withdraw His omnipotent, preserving hand from me, I should at once show what I am capable of when left to myself, by returning immediately into my nothingness. And, in the order of grace, the nothingness into which I relapse when left to myself is sin. How often "I am brought to nothing, and I knew not." (*Ps.* 72:22). And what can I find to be proud of in that nothingness?

Give me grace, O my God, to know myself, only as much as is necessary to keep me humble! For if I fully realized the insignificance of my own being and the extent of my malice, which is capable of offending Thee in divers, inconceivable ways, I fear I should be so filled with horror at myself that I should give way to despair!

We have within ourselves, in our experience and feelings, a knowledge of how greatly our frail and fallen nature is inclined to evil. Today we go and confess certain of our faults, making the resolution not to fall into them again, and tomorrow, notwithstanding, we commit them once more.

At one moment we make up our minds to

acquire a certain virtue, and the next we do just the contrary by falling into the opposite vice. At the time when we make these resolutions of amendment, we imagine that our will is firm and strong, but we soon perceive how weak and unreliable it is, for we behave as though we had never purposed amendment at all.

Our heart is like a reed that bends before every wind, or a barque tossed by every wave. It is sufficient to meet with an occasion of sin, a movement of passion, a breath of temptation, for the will to yield to evil, even when in certain moments of fervor we seem most firmly rooted in good. This is a strong reason for us to be humble and not to presume anything of ourselves, praying to God continually, that He may deign to confirm in our hearts that which He works through His grace. "Confirm, O God, what Thou hast wrought in us." (*Ps.* 67:29).

Some masters of the spiritual life teach that it is better to divert our thoughts from certain heroic actions in which our weakness might lead us to doubt whether we should succeed or not; for example, if a persecutor should come and summon me either to renounce the Faith or to die, how should I act? Or if I were to receive a terrible public insult, should I practice patience or resentment? No, they say it is not well to indulge in such imaginings because our weakness may cause us to fall before the idea of such a trial. But should such thoughts arise, we can turn them to our good and use our very weakness to practice humility.

When such ideas occur, it would be well to say: I know what I ought to do on such and such an occasion, but I know not how far I can trust myself, because I know by personal experience that "my strength is weakened through poverty," (*Ps.* 30:11), and I have learned on several occasions how my reason becomes blinded, my judgment weakened, and my will often perverted easily to evil. O my God, I can do all things if I am strengthened by Thy help; but without this, I can do nothing, nor shall I ever be able to do anything! If I had to confess Thee, I should miserably deny Thee; if to honor Thee by patience, I should give way to vengeance; if I had to obey Thee, I should offend Thee by disobedience. "Thou art a strong helper: when my strength shall fail, do not Thou forsake me." (*Ps.* 70:7, 9). Thy saying is quite true, O my God: "Without Me you can do nothing." (*John* 15:5). Not only without Thee can I never do any meritorious act of virtue whatsoever, but I cannot do anything at all; as St. Augustine instructs me: "Whether it be little or whether it be great, it cannot be done without Him without whom nothing can be done."[7]

15. A beautiful way of asking humility of God was the following, which was used by a great Saint: Lord, he said, I do not even know what humility is like, but I know that I do not possess

---

7. *"Sive parum sive multum sine illo fieri non potest."* (Tract. 31 in Joan.)

it and cannot of myself obtain it, and that unless I have it, I shall not be saved; therefore, it only remains for me to ask it of Thee; but give me the grace to ask it as I ought. Thou hast promised, O my God, to grant me all those things which I shall ask of Thee and which are necessary to my eternal salvation; and humility being most necessary to me, faith compels me to believe that Thou wilt grant me this, if I know how to ask it of Thee. But herein lies the difficulty, because I know not how to ask Thee as I ought. Teach me and help me that I may pray to Thee as Thou dost wish me to pray and in that efficacious manner in which Thou Thyself knowest that I shall be heard. And as Thou commandest me to be humble, I am ready to obey; but grant that, through Thy help, I may in truth become such as Thou dost desire. I ardently desire to be humble, and from whence comes this love and desire for humility, if not from Thee, who hast put it into my heart by Thy holy grace? Oh, of Thy goodness, grant me therefore what Thou hast made me to love and desire. I hope for it, and I will continue to hope for it. "Strengthen me, O Lord God, that, as Thou hast promised, I may bring to pass that which I have purposed, having a belief that it might be done by Thee." (*Judith* 13:7).

16. We may persuade ourselves that we possess various virtues because we have a tangible proof within us that we really have them. Thus we may judge ourselves to be chaste, because we feel

really attracted to chastity; or we may think ourselves abstemious, because we are so by nature;
or obedient, because we practice a ready obedience. But however much a man may exercise
humility, he can never form any judgment as to
his being really humble, for he who thinks himself
to be humble is no longer so.

In the same way that to recognize that we are
proud is the beginning of humility, so to flatter
ourselves that we are humble is the beginning of
pride, and the more humble we think ourselves,
the greater is our pride. That self-complacency
which the heart feels, making us imagine that we
are humble in consequence of some agreeable
reflections we have had about ourselves, is a
species of vanity; and how can vanity exist with
humility, which is founded solely on truth? Vanity
is nothing but a lie, and it is precisely from a lie
that pride springs.

Let us pray to God with the prophet: "Let not
the foot of pride come to me." (*Ps.* 35:12). Grant, O
my God, that I may be humble, but that I may not
know that I am humble. Make me holy, yet ignorant of holiness; for if I should learn to know or
even to imagine myself holy, I should become
vain, and through vanity should lose all humility
and holiness.

17. From what has just been said, it is possible
that a tormenting doubt might arise in the mind
of someone who might say: If I must judge myself
to be wanting in humility, I must conclude that I

am lost, and such a judgment would lead me to despair. But do you not perceive the error? To speak wisely, you ought to say: I know I am wanting in humility; therefore, I must try to obtain it, for without humility, I am a reprobate, and it is necessary to be humble in order to be among the elect.

There would indeed be cause for despair if, on the one hand, humility were necessary for salvation and, on the other, it were unattainable. But nothing is more natural to us than humility, because we are drawn toward it by our own misery; and nothing is easier, since it is enough for us to open our eyes and to know ourselves; this is not a virtue we need go far to seek, as we can always find it within ourselves, and we have an infinity of good reasons in ourselves for doing so. Nevertheless, we must labor as long as life lasts to acquire humility, nor must we ever imagine that we have acquired it; and even should we have obtained it in some degree, we must still continue to strive after it as though we did not possess it, in order that we may be able to keep it. Let us have a true desire to be humble; let us not cease to implore God that He may give us the grace to be humble; and let us often study the motives that may help to make us humble of heart; and let us not doubt the divine Goodness, but conform to the advice given us in Holy Writ: "Think of the Lord in goodness." (*Wisdom* 1:1).

18. Although we feel the humiliation keenly

when we are insulted, persecuted or calumniated, this does not mean that we cannot suffer such trials with sentiments of true humility, subjecting nature to reason and faith and sacrificing the resentment of our self-love to the love of God. We are not made of stone, so that we need be insensible or senseless in order to be humble. Of some martyrs we read that they writhed under their torments; of others, that they more or less rejoiced in them, according to the greater or lesser degree of unction they received from the Holy Ghost; and all were rewarded by the crown of glory, as it is not the pain or the feeling that makes the martyr, but the supernatural motive of virtue. In the same way some humble persons feel pleasure in being humiliated, and some feel sadness, especially when weighed down with calumny; and yet they all belong to the sphere of the humble, because it is not the humiliation nor the suffering alone which makes the soul humble, but the interior act by which this same humiliation is accepted and received through motives of Christian humility, and especially of a desire to resemble Jesus Christ, who though entitled to all the honors the world could offer Him, bore humiliation and scorn for the glory of His eternal Father: "O God of Israel, for Thy sake, I have borne reproach." (*Ps.* 68:8).

The doctrine of St. Bernard is worthy of our notice: It is one thing to be humiliated and another to be humble. It often happens that the proud man is humiliated, yet he nevertheless remains proud, receiving humiliations with anger and contempt, doing all he can to escape them with fretful impatience. It sometimes happens too that the proud man becomes humble, the humiliation teaching him to know himself as he is, and by this knowledge he learns to love this very humiliation: "He is humble who converts all his humiliations into humility and says unto God: 'It is good for me that Thou hast humbled me.'"[8]

19. In the spiritual life, I can promise myself nothing without the special help of God; and most true is the teaching of the Holy Ghost: "Thy help is only in Me." (*Osee* 13:9). From one moment to another, I may fall into mortal sin: consequently, even though I may have labored many years in acquiring virtues, I may in one instant lose all the good I have done, lose all my merit for eternity, and lose even that blessed eternity itself. How can a king rule with arrogance when he is besieged by his enemies and from day to day runs the risk of losing his kingdom and ceasing to be a king? And has not a saint abundant reasons, from the thought of his own weakness, to live always in a state of great humility, when he knows that from one hour to another he may lose the grace of God and the kingdom of Heaven, which he has merited by years of laboriously acquired virtues? "Unless

---

8. *"Est autem humilis qui humiliationem convertit in humilitatem, et dicit Deo: Bonum mihi quia humiliasti me."* (D. Bern. serm. 34 in *Cant.*)

the Lord build the house, they labor in vain that build it." (*Ps.* 126:1).

However spiritual and holy a man may be, he cannot regard himself as absolutely secure. The Angels themselves, enriched with sanctity, were not safe in Paradise. Man, endowed with innocence, was not safe in his earthly paradise. What safety, therefore, can there be for us with our corrupt nature, amid so many perils and so many enemies, who within and without are ever seeking insidiously to undermine our own eternal salvation?

In order to be eternally damned, it is enough that I should follow the dictates of nature; but to be saved, it is necessary that divine grace should prevent [go before] and accompany me, should follow and help me, watch over me and never abandon me. Oh, how right therefore was St. Paul in exhorting us to "work out our salvation"—which is for all eternity—"with fear and trembling!" (*Phil.* 2:12).

20. To be contented and self-satisfied, to lead a quiet, easy-going life, accomplishing only what duty prescribes, is not a good sign. After having done all that our Christian profession requires of us, Our Lord nevertheless wishes us to consider ourselves useless servants of His Church: "So you also, when you shall have done all these things that are commanded you, say: We are unprofitable servants." (*Luke* 17:10). Therefore how much more useless we ought to consider ourselves if we live in tepidity and sloth—by which we are still so far removed from that perfection to which we are bound!

When I make my examen of conscience, do I find that I fulfill all my duties in the sight of God? What virtue have I acquired hitherto? It may be said that we have acquired the habit of such and such a virtue when we come to practice it willingly and with facility; but when I examine myself, what virtue can I find which I habitually practice with pleasure and facility? I cannot find even one. I am a most unprofitable servant on earth; and if I were now called before the tribunal of my Eternal Judge, I must fear that it would be said to me: "Thou wicked servant," (*Matt.* 18:32), and not, "Well done, thou good and faithful servant." (*Matt.* 25:21).

21. In a country where all are blind, it is sufficient for a man to have but one eye for him to be said to have good sight; and among a multitude of ignorant people, one need possess but a slight tinge of knowledge to acquire the reputation of being very learned; and in the same way, in this wicked and corrupt world, it is easy to flatter ourselves that we are good, if we are not quite so bad as many others. "I am not as the rest of men." (*Luke* 18:11). It was in this way that the Pharisee praised himself in the temple.

But in order to know ourselves as we really are, it is not worldly-minded people that we ought to compare ourselves to, but to Jesus Christ, who is the model for all those who are predestined. "See," says St. Paul to every one of us, quoting the words that were said to Moses, "See (saith he) that thou make all things according to the pattern that was shown thee on the mount." (*Heb.* 8:5).

How have I conformed my life to the life of the Incarnate Son of God, who came to teach me the way to Heaven by His example? Ascend, O my Soul, to the hill of Calvary, and gaze attentively upon thy crucified Saviour! To this each one of us must conform in his own state of life if he wishes to be saved—such being the decree of the eternal Father, that the predestined must "be made conformable to the image of His Son." (*Rom.* 8:29).

But can I truthfully and conscientiously say that I imitate Him? In what way? Let me examine myself. Ah, how different I am from Him! And what just cause I find in this examen to humble myself! In comparing myself with sinners, I think myself a saint; but in comparing myself with Jesus Christ, whom I ought to imitate, I am compelled to acknowledge that I am a sinner and a reprobate; and the only consolation left to me is to trust in the infinite mercy of God. "O God, my support, and my deliverer." (*Ps.* 143:2).

22. Read the lives of the Saints, and consider whose life your own most resembles: what degree of sanctity do you possess? If you were to die at this moment, to what part of Paradise would you think yourself destined? Perhaps among the innocents? No one is innocent who has committed even one mortal sin; and you, have you still in your soul your baptismal innocence? Perhaps, therefore, among the penitents? But where is your penitence when, far from seeking self-mortification, you seek in all things to please yourself? Do you think you deserve to be numbered among the martyrs? I will not speak of the shedding of blood; but where is even your patience to suffer only the slightest trouble or adversity in this miserable life? Do you judge yourself worthy to be ranked with the virgins? But are you pure in body and mind? St. Anthony, the abbot, after having labored many years to perfect himself in holiness by imitating the virtues of all the most illustrious anchorites, found much to humble himself when he heard of St. Paul, the first hermit, and felt that, in comparison to this holy man, he himself had nothing of the religious left in him. O my Soul, come also and compare thyself to the Saints. "Call to remembrance the works of the fathers, which they have done in their generations," (*Mach.* 2:51), and thou wilt find innumerable occasions for humbling thyself in perceiving how far thou art from holiness. It is all very well to say: I do nothing wrong. To be saved, it is not enough not to do evil, but one must also do good. "Decline from evil and do good." (*Ps.* 36:27). It is not enough not to be a sinner by profession, but it is necessary to be holy by profession. "Follow peace with all men, and holiness, without which no man shall see God." (*Hebrews* 12:14).

23. Examine those virtues which you imagine

that you possess. Have you prudence, temperance, fortitude, justice, modesty, humility, chastity, humbleness of spirit, charity, obedience and many other virtues that may be necessary or suitable to your condition? If you have a few of these, in what degree do you possess them?

But I will say more: and that is, examine yourself first, and see whether you really have this virtue that you think you possess. What I mean to say is this: Is it a real virtue, or perhaps only a disposition of your natural temperament, be it melancholy, sanguine or phlegmatic?[9] And even should this virtue be real, is it a Christian virtue or purely a human one? Every act of virtue which does not proceed from a supernatural motive, in order to bring us to everlasting bliss, is of no value. And in the practice of virtue, do you join to your external actions the inward and spiritual acts of the heart? O True Christian Virtues, I fear that in me you are nothing but beautiful outward appearances! I deserve the reproach of God's word: "Because thou sayest: I am rich and made wealthy and have need of nothing, and knowest not that thou art wretched and miserable and poor and blind and naked." (*Apoc.* 3:17). And in the same manner the counsel of St. Augustine is good for me, that it is better to think of those

---

9. *Melancholy* means sober, thoughtful, pensive (sad, serious, sorrowful). *Sanguine* means cheerful, hopeful, confident (enthusiastic, buoyant, animated). *Phlegmatic* means calm, composed, collected (placid, quiet, self-possessed).

virtues in which we are lacking, rather than of those which we possess. "I will humble myself more for those virtues which I lack than pride myself on those I possess."[10]

24. In order that an act of virtue be truly virtuous, it is necessary that it should be so in all its component parts, and if it be defective on one point only, it becomes vitiated at once. A depraved intention, a single thought of vanity at the beginning, middle or ending of any virtuous work is sufficient to corrupt and change it into an evil one. It is enough for virtue to be wanting in humility for this virtue—which is no longer humble—to cease to be a virtue and to become a cause of mortal pride.

It often happens to one who leads a spiritual life that the more he strives after virtue, the more he finds a sweet pleasure in himself, and therefore, as St. Augustine says, the sole fact of his self-satisfaction quickly renders him displeasing to God. "The more man thinks he has reason to be pleased with himself, so much the more, I fear, his self-esteem will displease God, who resists the proud."[11]

Oh, how poor we seem when we examine our own spirituality and goodness by the help of these

---

10. *"Ero humilior ex eo quod deest quam elatior ex eo quod adest."* (*Ps.* 38).
11. *"Quo magis inest unde sibi placeat, eo magis vereor ne, sibi placendo, illi displiceat qui resistit superbis."* (*Lib. de Sancta Virginit.,* c. 34).

reflections! May it please God that we may not be like those men who, dreaming that they possess great riches, awaken at the point of death to find that they are only beggars. "They have slept their sleep: and all the men of riches have found nothing in their hands." (*Ps.* 75:6). May it please God that the plea of our virtue may not prove an argument for our greater condemnation. "And may that which is thought to be progress in virtue not prove to be a cause of damnation,"[12] says St. Gregory.

25. Humility is like purity: however little it may be contaminated, it becomes impure. Purity is corrupted not only by an impure act, but also by an immodest word or thought. And humility is also so fragile that it is easily tainted by the love of praise, by a word or thought of self-esteem, by vainglory or self-love.

He who really loves purity, not only diligently banishes all impure fancies, but also does so with horror and abomination; and in the same way, he who really loves humility, far from taking pleasure in praise and honor, is displeased by them, and instead of fleeing from humiliations, embraces them.

Oh, how much I find to humble myself here, for I see from this that I have no real love of humility! What is the result? One does not esteem a

---

12. "*Et non sit causa damnationis quod profectus putatur esse virtutis.*" (*Lib.* 5, Moral. c. 6).

virtue which one does not love, and one has but little desire to acquire a virtue which one neither esteems nor loves; and if this be the case, woe is me! If I have neither love nor esteem for humility, it is because I do not know how precious this virtue is in itself, nor how necessary it is to me. But, O my God, breathe over me that almighty word: "Be light made," (*Gen.* 1:3), so that I may be enlightened and learn to know this important virtue, which Thou dost desire that I should love. And with Thine aid, I will love it and guard it jealously, if I have light to understand it.

26. Every morning we ought to make this prayer and daily offering to God: "I offer Thee, O my God, all my thoughts, all my words and all my actions of this day. Grant that they may be thoughts of humility, words of humility and actions of humility—all to Thy glory."

Also during the course of the day, it will be well to repeat this ejaculatory prayer: "Lord Jesus, give me a humble and contrite heart." These few words contain all that we can possibly ask of God, because in praying for a contrite heart, we ask Him for that which is necessary to ensure forgiveness for our past life, and in praying for a humbled heart, all that which is required to secure life everlasting. Oh, may I at the hour of death find myself with a contrite and humbled heart! Then what confidence shall I not have in the mercy of God, if I can exclaim with King David: "A contrite and humble heart, O God, Thou wilt not despise." (*Ps.* 50:19). We very often offer prayers to God to which He might justly reply: "Thou knowest not what thou askest." But when we ask for holy humility, we know for certain we are asking for something which is most pleasing to God and most necessary to ourselves. And in asking for this, we must believe that God will maintain His infallible promise: "Ask, and it shall be given you." (*Matt.* 7:7).

27. If we examine all our falls into sin, whether venial or mortal, the cause will always be found in some hidden pride; and true indeed are the words of the Holy Ghost: "For pride is the beginning of all sin." (*Ecclus.* 10:15). Of this truth our Lord Jesus Christ Himself has warned us in His Gospel, where He says: "And whosoever shall exalt himself shall be humbled." (*Matt.* 23:12). God can give no greater humiliation to a soul than to allow it to fall into sin, because sin is the lowest depth of all that is base, vile and ignominious.

Therefore, each time that we are humbled by falling into sin, it is certain that we must previously have exalted ourselves by some act of pride, because only the proud are threatened with the punishment of this humiliation: "And he humbled himself afterwards, because his heart had been lifted up." (*2 Par.* 32:26). For thus it is written of King Ezechias in Holy Scripture, and the inspired writer has also said: "Before destruction, the heart of man is exalted." (*Prov.* 18:12).

There never has been a case of sin, says St. Augustine, nor ever will be one, nor can ever be one, of which pride was not in some measure the occasion: "There never can have been, and never can be, and there never shall be any sin without pride."[13]

Let us be so truly humble that we may not incur the punishment of this humiliation. No one can fall who lies on the ground, and no one can sin so long as he is humble. My God! My God! Let me remain in my nothingness, for it is the surest state for me.

28. We read of many who, after being renowned for their holiness, fervent in the exercise of prayer, great penances and signal virtues, and who after being favored by God with the gifts of ecstasy, revelations and miracles, have nevertheless fallen into the hideous vice of impurity at the slightest approach of temptation. And when I consider it, I find that there is no sin that degrades the soul so much as this impure sin of the senses, because the soul, from being reasoning and spiritual like the angels, becomes thereby carnal, sensual and like brute beasts "who have no understanding." (*Ps.* 31:9).

I am constrained to adore with fear the supreme judgments of God and also for my own warning to learn that pride was the reason of so

---

13. "*Nullum peccatum esse potuit aut potest aut poterit sine superbia.*" (*Lib. de Salute,* 19 *vel alias.*)

great a fall; therefore, we should all exclaim with the prophet, "And being exalted, I have been humbled and troubled," (*Ps.* 87:16), and say to ourselves the words which he said to Lucifer after he had "said in his heart, 'I will ascend,'" "How art thou fallen from heaven, O Lucifer." (*Is.* 14:13,12).

The soul is humbled according to the measure of its self-exaltation, and great must have been the pride which was followed by such a tremendous and abominable humiliation. Ah, how much more precious is one degree of humility in comparison to a thousand revelations or ecstasies! Of what use is it, says St. Augustine, to possess unsullied purity and chastity and virginity, if pride dominates the heart? "Of what avail is continence to him who is dominated by pride?"[14]

It is a wise and just disposition of God to permit the fall of the proud into every sin, and especially into that of wantonness, as being the most degrading, so that by so great a fall he should be ashamed, humbled and cured of his pride. O St. Thomas, how well hast thou said: "He who is fettered by pride and does not know it, falls into the sin of impurity, which is manifestly of itself disgraceful, that through this sin he may rise humiliated from his confession."[15] From this, the Saint continues, is shown the gravity of the sin of pride;

---

14. *"Quid prodest cui inest continentia, si dominatur superbia?"* (*Serm. de Verb. Dom.*).

15. *"Qui detinetur superbia et non sentit, labitur in carnis luxuriam quae manifeste per se turpis est; ut per hanc humiliatus a confusione exsurgat."* (22, Q. 161, art. 6, ad 3.).

and as a doctor often permits his patient to suffer from a minor ill in order to liberate him from a greater, so God permits the soul to fall into the sin of the senses, so that it may be cured of the vice of pride.

To whatever sublime height of sanctity we may have attained, a fall is always to be feared. For as St. Augustine says, there is no holiness that cannot be lost through pride alone: "If there be holiness in you, fear lest you may lose it. How? Through pride."[16]

However much our Christian self-love desires to avoid the remorse and repentance which ever follows the humiliations caused by sin, we should nevertheless desire and seek to be humble, because if we are humble, we can never be humbled. "O my Soul," we must say to ourselves, "O my Soul, look well into thyself and be humble if thou dost not will that God should humble thee with temporal and eternal shame." God promises to exalt the humble, and Heaven is filled with the humble. God also threatens the proud with humiliation, and Hell is filled with the proud. God thus promises and menaces so that if we do not remain in humility, allured by His great promises, we should at least remain in humility from fear of His potent threats: "And whosoever shall exalt himself shall be humbled, and he that shall humble himself shall be exalted." (*Matt.* 23:12).

---

16. "*Si est in vobis sanctitas, timete ne perdatis eam. Unde? Per superbiam.*" (*Serm. 13 de Verb. Dom.*).

God regards favorably the petitions of the humble and inclines to answer them: "He hath regard to the prayer of the humble, and He hath not despised their petition." (*Ps.* 101:18). But however much the proud man may invoke God, God will give him no spiritual consolation. St. Augustine says: "God will not come, even though thou call upon him, if thou art puffed up."[17]

These things are all old and oft-repeated, but it is because we know them and do not practice them that we deserve the reproof given by the prophet Daniel to Nabuchodonosor: "Thou hast not humbled thy heart, whereas thou knewest all these things." (*Dan.* 5:22).

30. At times we are over-scrupulous about works of supererogation [i.e., beyond our duty], such, for instance, as having omitted on such a day to say a certain prayer or to perform some self-imposed mortification; these are scruples of omissions, which in regard to our eternal salvation are of little or no importance. Yet we take but little heed of that humility which is to us most essential and necessary and without which no one can be saved. St. Paul warns us: "Do not become children in sense." (*1 Cor.* 14:20). Do not be like children who cry and despair if an apple is taken away from them, but care little for losing a gem of great value. Let us place humility above all things. It is

---

17. *"Deus venire non vult invocatus, si tu fueris elatus."* (*Enarr. in Ps.* 74.).

the hidden treasure buried in the field, to acquire which we ought to sell all we possess. (Cf. *Matt.* 13:44). It is the pearl of great price, to obtain which we should sell all we have. (Cf. *Matt.* 13:46).[18]

Do not let us call these sins against humility scruples, but let us regard them as real sins, worthy of Confession and of amendment. May God guard us from too easy a conscience in respect to that true humility which is commanded us in the Gospel. [Otherwise,] We should indeed be taking the broad way mentioned by the Holy Ghost, which though it seems the right and straight road, nevertheless leads directly to perdition: "There is a way that seemeth to a man right, and the ends thereof lead to death." (*Prov.* 16:25).

There are people who think like the Pharisees, that virtue and sanctity consist in prayers of great length, in the visiting of churches, and in some special abstinence, in retreats, in modesty of attire, in spiritual conferences or in some exercise of exterior piety. But in all this, who thinks of humility? Who esteems it and studies to acquire it? What is all this, then, but a vain delusion.

31. We read of various ancient philosophers who bore calumny, insults and contempt with perfect equanimity and without anger or perturbation,

---

18. The "treasure hidden in a field" and the "pearl of great price" spoken of by Our Lord refer primarily to the True Faith, but secondarily they may be understood of humility.

but they did not even know the name of humility. Their courageous fortitude was only an effect of refined pride, for as they considered themselves far above kings and emperors, they cared little about insults and maintained their equanimity by the contempt with which they looked down on those who insulted them. They overcame their feeling of resentment by a passion that was more dominating still; and that they were modest, peaceable and gentle was an effect of that pride which despotically ruled the feelings of their hearts.

There is an immense difference between the morality of human philosophy and that evangelical morality taught by Jesus Christ. Read the works of Seneca attentively—he who was held to exceed all other philosophers in morality—and you will see how, in those very maxims with which he teaches magnanimity and fortitude, he also instills pride. Read the works of the most famous of the Stoics, and you will say with St. Jerome that, "When they are studied with the greatest care and attention, there is to be found no satisfactory fullness of truth, no correspondence with the true principles of justice." [19]

All is vanity that only inspires vanity.

It is only in the Gospel of Jesus Christ that are to be found the rules of that humility of heart

---

19. *"Ubi cum summo studio fuerint ac labore perlecta, nulla ibi saturitas veritatis, nulla refectio justitiæ reperitur."* (*Epist.* 146, *ad Damas.*).

which is true virtue, consisting in the knowledge of God's greatness and of our own nothingness; and it is by attending to the study of this wise humility that we fulfill the apostolic precept: "Not to be more wise than it behoveth to be wise, but to be wise unto sobriety." (*Rom.* 12:3).

Jesus Christ, before teaching anything of His new law, wished to teach humility, as St. John Chrysostom observes: "When He began to lay down His divine laws, He started with humility."[20] For without humility it is impossible to comprehend this heavenly doctrine, but with humility we are enabled to understand everything that is necessary or useful to our salvation.

32. To confess our unworthiness and nothingness and to proclaim that all that is good in us comes from God is often the sterile exercise of a very contemptible humility, and may even be great pride, *"magna superbia,"* as St. Augustine observes. And St. Thomas teaches: "Humility, which is a virtue, is always fruitful in good works."[21]

Do you wish to have an idea of what that humility is which is a true virtue? The soul is truly humble when it recognizes that its true position in the order of nature or of grace is entirely dependent on the power, providence and

---

20. *"Incipiens divinas leges ab humilitate incepit."* (Hom. 39 *in Matt.*).
21. *S.T.,* IIa IIae, Q. 161, art. 5, ad 4.

mercy of God; so that finding in itself nothing but what is of God, it appropriates to itself only its own nothingness, and abiding in its nothingness, it places itself on the level of all other creatures, without raising itself in any way above them. It annihilates itself before God, not in order to remain in an otiose [idle] inactivity, but seeking rather to glorify Him continually, conforming with exact obedience to His laws and with perfect submission to His Will.

Humility has two eyes: with one we recognize our own misery, in order not to attribute to ourselves anything but our nothingness; with the other, we recognize our duty to work and to attribute everything to God, referring all things to Him: "Not to us, O Lord, not to us; but to Thy name give glory." (*Ps.* 113:1).

The truly humble man considers that whatever is good in his material or spiritual nature is like unto the streams that have come originally from the sea and must eventually return to the sea, and therefore he is always careful to render to God all that he has received from God, and neither prays for nor loves nor desires anything except that in all things the name of God be sanctified: "Hallowed be Thy name." (*Matt.* 6:9).

33. Humility is not a sickly virtue, timid and feeble, as some imagine; on the contrary, it is strong, magnanimous, generous and constant, because it is founded on truth and justice. The truth consists in knowing what God is and what we are. Justice consists in our recognizing that God, as our Creator, has a right to command us and that we, as His creatures, are bound to obey Him.

All the martyrs were perfectly humble because they preferred to die, suffering the most terrible torments, rather than abandon truth and justice. How great their endurance and courage in resisting those who tried to force them to deny Jesus Christ!

To contradict others is an effect of pride, whenever we contradict them in order to follow our own unjust and mistaken will; but when our opposition to the creature proceeds from a determination to fulfill the will of the Creator, it is dictated by humility; for by this we confess our indispensable obligation to be subject and obedient to the divine Will.

It is for this reason that the proud man is always timid, because his pride is only sustained by the weakness of human nature. And he who is humble is always brave in the exercise of his submission to the Divine Majesty, because he receives his strength through grace.

The humble obey men, when in so doing they also obey God; but they refuse obedience to men, when by obeying them they would disobey their God. Reflect upon that answer, as modest as it was magnanimous, given before the elders of Jerusalem by St. Peter and St. John: "If it be just in the sight of God to hear you rather than God, judge ye." (*Acts* 4:19).

The humble man is above all human respect,

and there is no danger that he will become a slave to the opinions, fashions or customs of the world; he knows his failings and that he is capable of every evil, even though he does not commit it. If he sees others doing wrong, he compassionates them, but is never scandalized or induced to follow the bad examples of others, because all his intentions are directed toward God, and he has no other desire than that of pleasing God and of being directed by God alone. "He clings to God alone." Hence, as the angelic St. Thomas says so well: "No matter how much he sees others acting inordinately in word or deed, he himself will not depart from his uprightness of conduct."[22]

34. The heart of the proud man is like a stormy sea, never at rest: "Like the raging sea, which cannot rest." (*Is.* 57:20). And the heart of the humble is fully content in its humility—"Rich in his being low" (*James* 1:10)—and is always calm and tranquil and without fear that anything in this world should disturb him, and shall "rest with confidence." (*Is.* 14:30). And from whence proceeds this difference? The humble man enjoys peace and quiet because he lives according to the rules of truth and justice, submitting his own will in all things to the Divine Will. The proud man is always agitated and perturbed because of the

---

22. "*Soli Deo inhæret; unde, quantumcumque videat alios inordinate se habere dictis vel factis, ipse a sua rectitudine non recedit.*" (*S.T.,* IIa IIae, Q. 33, art. 5).

opposition he is continually offering to the Divine Will in order to fulfill his own.

The more the heart is filled with self-love, so much the greater will be its anxiety and agitation. This maxim is indeed true; for whenever I feel myself inwardly irritated, disturbed and angered by some adversity which has befallen me, I need not look elsewhere for the cause of such feelings than within myself, and I should always do well to say: If I were truly humble, I should not be disquieted. My great agitation is an evident proof which ought to convince me that my self-love is great and dominant and powerful within me, and is the tyrant which torments and gives me no peace.

If I feel aggrieved by some sharp word that has been said to me, or by some discourtesy shown to me, from whence does this feeling of pain proceed? From my pride alone. Oh, if I were truly humble, what calm, what peace and happiness would my soul not enjoy! And this promise of Jesus Christ is infallible: "Learn of Me, because I am meek and humble of heart, and you shall find rest to your souls." (*Matt.* 11:29).

When we are distressed by some adversity, it is unnecessary to seek consolation from those who flatter us or have pity on us, and to whom we can pour out our troubles. It is sufficient to ask our soul: "Why art thou cast down, O my Soul? And why dost thou disquiet me?" (*Ps.* 41:12). My Soul, what hast thou? And what seekest thou? Dost thou perchance desire that rest which thou hast lost? Listen then to the remedy offered to thee by thy Saviour, exhorting thee to learn of Him to be humble, "Learn of Me, because I am meek and humble of heart," and further listen to what He adds when He assures thee that with thy lost humility thou shalt also recover thy peace: "And you shall find rest to your souls." (*Matt.* 11:29).

35. There are two kinds of humiliation: those which we seek of our own free will and those which proceed from the natural and temporal vicissitudes of this life. Against the first we must be on our guard, notwithstanding the ardor with which we embrace them, for the ever-lurking vanity of our self-love is so subtle that it seeks even to enhance its own vainglory, while it appears to seek the contempt of man. But if we accept the other humiliations which come to us, irrespective of our will, mortifying our feelings, thoughts and passions with prompt resignation to the Will of God, it is a sign of true and sincere humility, because such humiliations tend to mortify our self-love and to perfect the submission which we owe to God.

Voluntary and self-sought humiliations may cause the soul to become hypocritical. But involuntary humiliations, sent to us by the Divine Will, and borne by us with patience, sanctify the soul. And for this reason the Holy Ghost has given us this most important mandate: "In thy humiliation keep patience. For gold and silver are tried in the fire, but acceptable men in the furnace of humiliation." (*Ecclus.* 2:4-5). It is impossible, except in rare cases, not to discover the hypocrisy of affected humility: "Touch the mountains, and they shall smoke." (*Ps.* 143:5). And again, it is impossible not to know the virtue of true humility, because its spirit is "gentle, kind, steadfast, assured, secure, having all power." (*Wis.* 7:23).

36. There are also two kinds of temptation: those that come to us through the wickedness of the evil one and those which we go in search of ourselves in our own weakness and malice. But against either there is no better safeguard than humility. Humility causes the evil one to flee, because he cannot face the humble, on account of his great pride, and it causes every temptation to vanish suddenly because there can be no temptation without a touch of pride.

Temptations arise against purity or against faith or any other virtue, but we can easily overcome them if we humble ourselves in our hearts and say: "Lord, I deserve these terrible temptations as a punishment for my pride, and if Thou dost not come to my help, I shall surely fall. I feel my weakness, and that I can do no good of myself. Help me!" "O God, come to my assistance; O Lord, make haste to help me." (*Ps.* 69:2).

The more a soul humbles itself before God, the more God comforts that soul with His grace; and inasmuch as God is with us, who shall prevail against us? "The Lord is the protector of my life, of whom shall I be afraid?" (*Ps.* 26:1) said King

David; and St. Paul said: "If God be for us, who is against us?" (*Rom.* 8:31).

The strongest subterfuge which the devil can employ in order to make us fall into temptation is to flatter our humility, thus preventing us from being humble. For if the evil one succeeds in persuading us that we have sufficient strength of ourselves to overcome temptation, we have already succumbed, as those succumbed of whom it was written that the Lord humbleth "them that presume of themselves and glory in their own strength." (*Judith* 6:15).

Charity never grows cold nor fervor tepid, except from lack of humility. Let us stand on our guard, clad in the armor of humility, and that will be sufficient. God will help us in the measure in which we are humble, and with His help we shall be able to say: "I can do all things in Him who strengtheneth me." (*Phil.* 4:13).

37. As for those other temptations there must certainly be presumption on our part when we seek them of our own accord and place ourselves in dangerous occasions of sin. He who is humble knows his own weakness, and knowing it, fears to place himself in danger; and because he fears it, he flees from it. He who is humble trusts implicitly in the help of divine grace on those involuntary occasions he may encounter, but he never presumes upon the help of divine grace on those occasions which he has sought himself.

Let us be humble, and humility will teach us to

fear and to avoid all dangerous occasions. In the lives of the Saints, we read how careful they were to avoid familiar intercourse with women; and also in the lives of saintly women, how equally cautious they were to avoid familiarity with men. Why did they fear so much, since they already had so many penances and prayers with which to defend themselves against temptation? The reason is that they were humble and distrusted the weakness of human nature, without presuming on grace; and thus their humility was the means by which they kept their purity unsullied.

You say: I can put myself in the way of temptation, but I am not afraid because I will not sin. This is a temerity proceeding from pride; as St. Thomas says: "This is a real temerity and it is caused by pride,[23] and you would find yourself shamed by an unexpected fall. "And he that loveth danger shall perish in it." (*Ecclus.* 3:27). All that presume thus will undoubtedly fall, and their fall is the just punishment of their pride, as the prophet predicted: "This shall befall them for their pride." (*Soph.* 2:10).

38. God resists the proud, because the proud oppose Him; but He dispenses His graces liberally to the humble, because they live in subjection to His Will. Oh, if we humbly made place for the divine gifts, how great would be the affluence of

---

23. *"Hoc proprie temeritas est quæ causatur ex superbia."* (*S.T.,* IIa IIae, Q. 53, art. 3, ad 2.).

that grace in our souls! One of the worst conse-
quences of our lack of humility will be that it will
render the Day of Judgment so terrible to us,
because on that day we shall not only have to give
account of the graces which we have received and
of which we have made a bad use, but also of
those graces which God would have given us if we
had been humble and which He withheld from us
on account of our pride.

It will be useless then to excuse ourselves by
saying that we fell into such and such a sin from
want of grace. "Grace was there," the Lord will
answer; "but you ought to have asked for it with
humility and not forfeited it by your pride." Pride
is an obstacle harder than steel, which hinders
the beneficent infusion of grace into the soul. And
it is the doctrine of St. Thomas that it is precisely
by pride that our soul is placed in such a state "as
to be deprived of all inner spiritual good."[24] Do
you desire grace in this world and glory in the
next? Humble yourself, says St. James: "Be humbled in the sight of the Lord, and He will exalt
you." (*Jas.* 4:10). God created out of nothing all
that we can see in our world when "the earth was
void and empty," (*Gen.* 1:2), and He filled with oil
all the empty vases with which the widow pre-
sented Eliseus: "Empty vessels not a few." (*4 Kgs.*
4:3). And He also fills with His grace those hearts
which are emptied of self—that is to say, which

---

24. *"Per hoc quod privatur interioribus bonis."* (*S.T.,* IIa IIae,
Q. 132, art. 3).

have neither self-esteem nor self-confidence and do not rely upon their own strength.

It is most humiliating to reflect upon this, that even though we be exempt from grave sins, yet through some secret disorder within us, we may be as guilty as if we had committed them. For if pride arises in our hearts and leads us to consider ourselves better than those who have committed these sins, we are at once rendered guilty and worse than they in the eyes of God, because, as the Holy Ghost says, "Pride is hateful before God." (*Ecclus.* 10:7). St. Luke in his Gospel (*Luke* 18:11-12) records two different kinds of vanity shown by the Pharisee, one when he praised himself for the sins he did not commit, the other when he praised himself for the virtues that he practiced: and he was equally condemned for each of these vain utterances. He apparently referred all the glory to God when he said: "O God, I give Thee thanks." But this was only ostentatious self-esteem. It is only too easy for these thoughts of vainglory to insinuate themselves into our hearts, and who can assure me that I am not guilty of many of them? "What I have done openly I see," I can say with more truth than St. Gregory, "but what I have inwardly felt I do not see."[25] O my God, my God, "let no iniquity have dominion over me." (*Ps.* 118:133). Do not let me be dominated by pride, which is the sum of all wickedness; from my

---

25. "*Quae aperte egerim video, quid in his latenter pertulerim ignoro.*" (*Lib.* 9, *Mor.,* c. 17).

secret sins cleanse me. Purify me from those sins of pride of which I am ignorant; "then shall I be without spot." (*Ps.* 18:14). This thought, says St. Thomas, causes every just man to consider himself worse than a great sinner: "The just man who is truly humble thinks himself worse because he fears lest in that which he seems to do well he should grievously sin by pride."[26]

40. It may be said that humility is the most efficacious remedy for all evil and a most potent antidote to preserve the soul from that death and guilt which leads to everlasting perdition. And yet it is this virtue which we neglect most of all.

O my Soul, God, who Himself desires thine eternal salvation, desires also that thou shouldst acquire it through humility. "And humility goeth before glory." (*Prov.* 15:33). Therefore, bow down and adore His sovereign Will. When we say the "Our Father," let us meditate upon that petition, in which we ask that the Will of God may be done, and let us apply that prayer to our own needs: O my God, since Thou desirest that I should be humble, "Thy Will be done." Thy Will is done in Heaven by all those blessed spirits who worship Thee with profound humility; may Thy Will be done by me also! "Thy Will be done on earth, as it is in Heaven." And in the same way, let us apply

---

26. "*Justus qui est vere humilis reputat se deteriorem, quia timet ne in his quæ bene agere videtur per superbiam gravius delinquat.*" (in suppl. 3 part. Q. 6, art. 4).

the last petition to ourselves also, saying: "And deliver us from evil," praying God to deliver us and preserve us from pride, which is the worst of all evils, if indeed it may not be called the greatest of all sins. For St. Augustine, inquiring into which sin King David desired most to be delivered from when he said, "I shall be cleansed from the greatest sin," (*Ps.* 18:14), answers that this sin was pride, for pride is the greatest of all sins because it is the chief of all sins and the cause and origin of them all: "This I take to be pride, which is the chief and cause of every sin."[27]

41. We may say that one of the principal causes of our lack of humility is that we forget too readily the sins we have committed. We only think of our sins when we are preparing for Confession, and even then we only think of our sins in order to sum up their kind and number, in order to make a valid Confession, but we hardly ever stop to consider their gravity, enormity and malice. And even if we do bestow some slight thought on them, it is only in order to flatter ourselves that our sorrow is sufficient for the validity of our Confession; and what is still more amazing is that we are hardly out of the confessional when the remembrance of all our sins vanishes, and even the greatest sinner lives in a state of absolute peace, as if he had always led the most innocent

---

27. *"Hoc arbitror esse superbiam, quæ caput et causa omnium delictorum est."* (Enarr. in *Ps.* 18).

of lives. O miserable state! We always retain a vivid remembrance of those insults which we receive from our fellow-men, thereby fostering our resentment; but we do not bear in remembrance those insults which we have offered to God, thereby becoming humble and exhorting ourselves to repentance. What wonder that we do not become humble, if we remain oblivious to these urgent motives for humility!

Let us remember our sins, not in order that they should make us overscrupulous, but in order to live in due humility. It is for that same reason that Jeremias the prophet said that he who does not do penance does not practice humility, because "There is none that doth penance for his sin, saying: What have I done?" (*Jer.* 8:6). If we thought well over this—"What have I done?" What have I done in sinning? What have I done in offending God?—our hearts would certainly be far more contrite and humble. But few think of this.

We call upon the heavens to be astonished at us: "Be astonished, O ye heavens, at this." (*Jer.* 2:12). If a nobleman is insulted in some public resort by a low-born menial, the offense is considered great, and an adequate punishment is demanded for such an outrage; and yet it is only a man who has been insulted by another man, a worm that is offended by another worm, nothingness offended by nothingness. But that this worm, this nothingness, should insult the Divine Majesty of God apparently causes no dismay. "Be astonished, O ye heavens," but at least let us be ashamed and humble ourselves for our insensate hardness of heart.

42. There are two special virtues which the Son of God wished to teach us and recommended us most earnestly to practice—humility and brotherly love. And it is precisely against these two virtues that the devil wages war the most. But it is enough that he should succeed in conquering humility for love to be overcome at the same time, because as St. Augustine says: "You cannot attain to charity except through humility."[28] Pride is always ready to take offense, and with this disposition to resent slights and injuries, how is it possible to live in charity? When we find two persons who are prone to disagree and to whom reconciliation is difficult, we cannot be far wrong in concluding that both are full of pride. Therefore, it is obvious that charity cannot exist without humility.

It is for this reason that St. Paul, after having exhorted Christians to brotherly love, advises them at the same time to be humble: "But in humility, let each esteem others better than themselves," (*Phil.* 2:3), for well he knew that brotherly love cannot endure without humility. For where pride exists, there will also arise contentions, quarreling and strife: "Among the proud there are always contentions." (*Prov.* 13:10).

---

28. *"Non pervenitur ad charitatem, nisi per humilitatem."* (Enarr. in *Ps.* 130, et serm. 10 *de Verbo Dom.*)

Let us accept the apostolic admonition, and do not let us blame others for their pride when they cause us displeasure, but rather blame ourselves for not knowing how to bear that displeasure with humility. Let us begin by acquiring that patient humility ourselves which we desire so much to see in others, remembering that it is not through the patience and humility of others that we shall be saved, but by our own.

43. It is difficult for those who possess riches or learning to be humble, because these two gifts are apt to cause vanity in those who possess them. It is far better, therefore, to be less rich and less learned and to be humble, than to possess great riches or great learning and to be proud.

Nevertheless, many who are now Saints in Heaven were both rich and learned when they were on earth; but they are Saints because they were humble; and both riches and learning must be regarded as vanity, and not esteemed except in so far as they can help us to gain eternal happiness. This is the way of the truly humble: he does not esteem himself for his possessions or for his knowledge, but regards these all as nothing, because he regards himself also as nothingness.

"Set not your heart upon them." (*Ps.* 61:11). This is not a counsel but a precept; and God, through His prophet, wishes to instruct us: If you are rich in possessions or in knowledge, be nevertheless poor of heart, that is to say, be humble. This is difficult, it is true; but to overcome the difficulty increases the merit of the virtue. There is no great merit in being humble when our condition is lowly, but there is great merit in being humble when we are surrounded by the incentives to pride, which are riches and learning. St. Bernard says: "It is no great thing for a man to be humble in abjection, but for one who is honored, humility is altogether a great and rare virtue."[29] It is a beautiful sight for men and for Angels to see a rich man who is modest and apparently forgetful of his wealth, and a wise man who seems unaware of his great knowledge.

44. Although sin is in itself a great evil—in fact the greatest of all evils—still, under a certain form, it can prove a good to us if we know how to avail ourselves of it as a means of exercising humility. How many great sinners have become great saints without having done anything more than to keep their sins constantly before their eyes and to humble themselves in shame and confusion before God and their fellowmen!

Those words: "Against Thee only have I sinned," which David carried in his heart, contributed more than anything else to make him a Saint. And the angelic St. Thomas—in explaining the verse of St. Paul to the Romans (*Rom.* 8:28) ["And we know that to them that love God, all

---

29. *"Non magnum est esse humilem in abjectione, magna prorsus et rara virtus est humilitas honorata."* (Hom. 4 *super "Missus est"*).

things work together unto good, to such as, according to his purpose, are called to be saints."]—says: "This is the good that profits them that love God, for when they fall from the love of God by sin, they then return to Him more humble and more cautious." [30]

It is in this that the goodness and wisdom of God is most admirably set forth, that He offers us a means of sanctifying ourselves through our very miseries, and we shall never be able to make the excuse that we could not become saints because we committed grave sin, when those very sins might have been the means of sanctifying us by urging us to a deeper humility. How great is God's mercy in thus giving me the means of sanctifying myself if only by remembering that I have sinned and by meditating, in the light of Holy Faith, upon what it means to be a sinner!

St. Mary Magdalen did not become holy so much by the tears she shed as by the humility of her heart. Her sanctification began when she first began to be humble in the knowledge of herself and of God. "She knew." (*Luke* 7:37). ["And behold a woman . . . a sinner, when she knew that he sat at meat in the Pharisee's house, brought an alabaster box of ointment; and standing behind at his feet, she began to wash his feet with tears and wiped them with the hairs of her head, and kissed

---

30. *"Diligentibus Deum proficit in bonum hoc ipsum quod per peccatum in Dei amore cadunt; quia humiliores redeunt et cautiores."* (*S.T.*, IIIa, Q. 89, art. 2 ad. 1).

his feet and anointed them with the ointment."
(*Luke* 7:37-38)].

She advanced in sanctity as she advanced in
humility, for when she did not dare to appear
before Jesus Christ, she remained behind Him,
"and standing behind," (*Luke* 7:38), and she com-
pleted her career of sanctity by her humility, for
as St. Gregory says, she did nothing all the rest of
her life but meditate upon the great evil she had
committed in sinning. "She considered what she
had done."[31]

45. When we feel ashamed and disturbed at having fallen into sin, this is but a temptation of the
devil, who tries to make use of our distress to
draw us perhaps into some graver sin.

The sorrow we feel at having offended God does
not distress the soul, but rather leaves it calm
and serene, because it is a sorrow united to
humility, which brings grace with it; but to be distressed and overwhelmed by sadness—either
from the shame we feel at having committed some
disgraceful action, or from a sudden recognition of
our liability to fall, just when we thought ourselves stronger and more faithful than ever—is
simply pride, which is born of an excessive self-
love. We have too good an opinion of ourselves,
and this is the reason why we are disturbed when
we see our reputation injured by others or diminished by our own actions. If I reflect well when-

---

31. *"Consideravit quid fecit."* (Hom. 20 in Evang.)

ever I am distressed about my own faults, I shall find that my distress is only due to pride, which persuades me, by the subtle artifice of self-love, that I am better than the just themselves, of whom it is written: "A just man shall fall seven times." (*Prov.* 24:16).[32]

He who is humble, even though he fall through frailty, soon repents with sorrow and implores the divine assistance to help him to amend; nor is he astonished at having fallen, because he knows that of himself he is only capable of evil and would do far worse if God did not protect Him with His grace. After having sinned, it is good to humble oneself before God, and without losing courage, to remain in humility in order not to fall again, and to say with David: "I have been humbled, O Lord, exceedingly; quicken Thou me according to Thy word." (*Ps.* 118:107). But to afflict ourselves without measure and to give way to a certain pusillanimous [cowardly] melancholy, which brings us to the verge of despair, is a temptation of pride, insinuated by the devil, of whom it is written, "he is king over all the children of pride." (*Job* 41:25).

46. However upright we may be, we must never

---

32. The meaning of "a just man" is one who is not in the state of mortal sin. He can still fall into venial sin—even seven times *or more* each day—and yet remain a just man. This is only basic Catholic moral theology. This point is simply another example that a person needs to know the Catholic Faith in order to understand Scripture.

be scandalized nor amazed at the conduct of evil-doers, nor consider ourselves better than they, because we do not know what is ordained for them or for us in the supreme dispositions of God, "Who doth great things and unsearchable and wonderful things without number." (*Job* 5:9).

When Zaccheus thought only of usury and oppressing the poor, when Magdalen filled Jerusalem with scandal, when Paul cursed and persecuted the Christian religion, who would have imagined that they would ever have become Saints? And on the other hand, who would have believed that Solomon, the oracle of divine wisdom, would die in the midst of wantonness and idols? That Judas, one of the Apostles, would betray his Divine Master and then give himself up to despair? Or that many holy men, advanced in sanctity, would have become apostates? These are examples which should make us tremble when we reflect upon the unfathomable mystery of the judgment and mercy of God: "One He putteth down, and another He lifteth up." (*Ps.* 74:8). "He hath put down the mighty from their seat, and hath exalted the humble." (*Luke* 1:52).

Every Saint can in a moment become a sinner if he is vain of his sanctity; and a sinner can as quickly become a Saint—if he is contrite and humbles himself for his sin. How many there are who in the fervor of their prayer "mount up to the heavens" and soon afterwards, at the slightest occasion of sin, "they go down to the depths!" (*Ps.* 106:26). How many there are too, who, given up to vanity and stained with the deepest sins, are suddenly changed by having their eyes opened to the knowledge of the truth and who thus attain to Christian perfection! Indeed, the high counsels of God are to be adored and not scrutinized, for "The Lord humbleth and exalteth; He raiseth up the needy from the dust, and lifteth up the poor from the dunghill." (*1 Kgs.* 2:7-8).

47. Who knows if the one I judge and speak ill of may not be dearer to God than I am? Whether another, whom I esteem but little and despise for his physical or moral defects, be not destined to be very happy with God for all eternity? Who knows whether I may not be condemned to the pains of Hell for all eternity? With this uncertainty, how can I then presume to consider myself better than any other?

No one is worth more than what he is worth in the eyes of God, and how can I know whether I am an object of hatred or of love to God? "And yet man knoweth not whether he be worthy of love or hatred." (*Eccles.* 9:1). How do I know if God will fashion a vessel of honor or of dishonor from the clay of which I am made? "For who distinguisheth thee?" (*1 Cor.* 4:7). "But what is the use of these vessels? the potter is the judge." (*Wis.* 15:7).

When I read of St. Paul, the herald of the Holy Ghost and great doctor of the Gentiles—who said of himself that he lived in fear of falling into sin and becoming a castaway after having converted so many thousands of souls to God ("Lest perhaps when I have preached to others, I myself may become a castaway," *1 Cor.* 9:27)—ah, if St. Paul himself should thus fear, who was rapt unto the third Heaven and could say that Christ lived in him, ("and I live now, not I, but Christ liveth in me," *Gal.* 2:20), what shall I say of myself, who am so contemptible? At the Day of Judgment, how many shall we see on the right hand of God whom we looked upon as castaways, and how many shall we see on His left, whom we believed to be among His elect!

It would be well for us, however, when we make comparisons between ourselves and others, to say what Juda said of Thamar, "She is juster than I," (*Gen.* 38:26), and in some circumstance or other this will always prove to be true. St. Thomas taught that a man may truthfully say and believe that he is worse than others, partly on account of the hidden defects which he knows that he possesses and partly on account of the gifts of God that are hidden in others.[33]

48. Who can assure me that before long I shall not fall into some mortal sin? And having once fallen, who can assure me that I may not die in sin and thus be condemned to eternal punishment? As long as I live in this world, I cannot be sure of anything. I must hope to save my soul, but

---

33. *"Aliquis absque falsitate potest se credere et pronunciare omnibus viliorem secundum defectus occultos quos in se recognoscit et dona Dei quæ in aliis latent."* (IIa IIae, Q. 161, art. 6, ad 2).

I must also fear to lose it. O my Soul, I do not intend to depress thee; no, nor do I wish to fill thee with pusillanimous [cowardly] despair by these thoughts. I only desire thee to be humble. And how much reason hast thou to humble thyself in this uncertainty, not knowing what manner of death shall be thine, nor what shall be thy lot for all eternity? It is only by the measure of thy humility that thou canst hope to please God and save thyself, because it is certain that God will "save the humble people," (*Ps.* 17:28), "and He will save the humble of spirit." (*Ps.* 33:19).

There are some who think that to meditate on the mystery of predestination is likely to fill us with despair; but it appears to me, as it also did to St. Augustine, that this thought is a most efficacious means of practicing humility,[34] because when I meditate upon my eternal salvation, I see that it does not depend [solely] upon the power of my own free-will [co-operating with God's grace], but [mainly] only upon the divine mercy. Not trusting to myself, but placing all my hope in God, I must say with the wise Judith: "And therefore let us humble our souls before Him, and continuing in a humble spirit in His service, ask the Lord . . . that He would show His mercy to us." (*Judith* 8:16-17).

49. It is a special gift of God to know how to govern the tongue, as the preacher says in his Proverbs: "It is the part . . . of the Lord to govern

---

34. *Lib. de Prædest. et Grat.*

the tongue," ["It is the part of man to prepare the soul, and of the Lord to govern the tongue."] (*Prov.* 16:1). And when God wishes to confer this gift of His upon anyone, He does so by means of humility. And the Savior teaches us in *St. Matthew:* "Out of the abundance of the heart the mouth speaketh." (*Matt.* 12:34). Therefore, if the heart is well-regulated by humility, the tongue will be well-regulated also.

He who is humble of heart has but a poor opinion of himself and a good opinion of others; hence it is that he never praises himself or blames others. The humble man speaks but little, and weighs and measures his words in order not to say more than truth and modesty require, and as his heart is free from vanity, so is his speech. We argue, therefore, that there can be little or no humility in our hearts when there is little or no circumspection in our speech. "Their heart is vain," says the prophet, and this is the reason why he also adds: "Their throat is an open sepulchre." (*Ps.* 5:10-11). We speak of those things that fill the heart, "For out of the abundance of the heart the mouth speaketh," (*Luke* 6:45), and our speech will determine whether truth or vanity predominates in our hearts. It is well to ask God to curb our tongue, but let us also ask Him to give humility to our heart, for this alone will be a most powerful curb.

50. Humility is charitable, interpreting all things for the best and pitying and excusing the faults of others as much as possible. For this reason St. Peter, wishing to exhort us to love and have compassion upon our fellow-creatures, also exhorts us at the same time to be humble: "Having compassion one of another, being lovers of the brotherhood [merciful, modest,] humble," (*1 Peter* 3:8), for there can be no charity without humility, and therefore to censure and criticize too readily the actions of our neighbors and to judge and speak ill of them are vices which are directly opposed to the virtue of humility. Who has given me the power to judge my brethren? When I thus constitute myself their judge and in the tribunal of my thoughts condemn first one and then another, I am usurping an authority I do not possess and which belongs to God alone: "For God is judge." (*Ps.* 49:6). And if this is not pride, what is pride? In punishment of such arrogance, God often permits us to fall into the very faults that we have condemned in others, and it is well for us to remember the teaching of St. Paul: "Wherefore thou art inexcusable, O man, whosoever thou art that judgest. For wherein thou judgest another, thou condemnest thyself." (*Rom.* 2:1). There is always some pharisaical pride in the heart of him who judges and speaks evil of others, because in belittling others, he exalts himself. It is in vain that we try to cover our evil-speaking under the veil of some good motive; it must always be the result of pride, which is quick to find out the weaknesses of others while remaining blind to its own.

If we are guilty of pride, let us try to amend and not to flatter ourselves that we possess the smallest degree of humility until, by our good resolutions carefully carried out, we have mortified our evil tendency to speak ill of our neighbor. Let us hearken to the Holy Ghost: "Where pride is, there also shall be reproach; but where humility is, there also is wisdom." (*Prov.* 11:2).

The proud man is scornful and arrogant in his speech, and the humble alone knows how to speak well and wisely. If there is humility in the heart, it will be manifested in the speech, because "A good man out of the good treasure of his heart bringeth forth that which is good." (*Luke* 6:45).

51. But in order to acquire humility, it is necessary also to be prudent in not speaking well of oneself. "Let another praise thee," says the Inspired Word, "and not thy own mouth: a stranger, and not thy own lips." (*Prov.* 27:2).

It is very easy for us to fall into this fault of praising ourselves, until it becomes a habit, and with this habit so opposed to humility, how can we be humble?

What good qualities have we of our own for which we can praise ourselves? All the good that is in us comes from God, and to Him alone we must give praise and honor. When, therefore, we praise ourselves, we are usurping glory, which is due to God alone. Even though in praising ourselves we sometimes refer all to the honor of God, it matters little; when there is no absolute necessity, it is better to abstain from self-praise, for although we refer all to the glory of God with our lips, our ingenious and subtle self-love cannot fail to appropriate it secretly. And even speaking depreciatingly of ourselves, there may lurk some hypocritical pride in our words, such as was mentioned by the sage of old when he said: "There is one that humbleth himself wickedly, and his interior is full of deceit." (*Ecclus.* 19:23).

Therefore, we can never watch over ourselves enough, because there is nothing that teaches us so well to know the pride of our heart as our own words, with which we either reveal or hide the depravity of our affections. And this is the characteristic of the proud, according to St. Bernard: "One who boastfully proclaims what he is, or lies about what he is not."[35]

Let us bear in heart and mind this precious advice given by Tobias to his son: "Never suffer pride to reign in thy mind or in thy words." (*Tobias* 4:14). The words of a proud man are nauseous, whether he speaks of himself or others, and they are hated both by God and man; therefore, we should detest this vice, not only from the Christian, but also from the human standpoint.

52. God has Himself given us the means of obtaining this humility of heart, in the remembrance of death and by meditation upon it. Death

---

35. *"Qui vel sibi arrogat quod est, vel mentitur de se quod non est."* (Epist. 87).

is the best teacher of truth; and pride—being nothing but an illusion of our heart—clings to a vanity which it does not recognize as vanity; and therefore death is the best means by which we can learn what vanity is and how to detach our hearts from it.

Our self-love is wounded at the thought that we must soon die, and when we least expect it, and that with death everything comes to an end for us in this world; but at the same time, this reflection weakens and humbles our self-love. Unfortunately, we do not think of death with that seriousness which we ought to give to it.

If I knew for certain that I had to die within a year, I imagine that I should grow more humble from day to day at the thought that each day was bringing me nearer to my death. But who can assure me that I have one year to live—I, who am not certain to live to the end of the day?

O my God, True Light of my soul, keep alive within me the remembrance of my death. Tell me often with Thine own voice in my heart that I must die, perhaps within a year, perhaps within a month, perhaps within a week; and thus I shall remain humble. In order that the thought of death may not be unfruitful to me, excite within my soul now that knowledge and those feelings which I shall have at that last hour of my life, when the blessed taper is placed in my hands "in the day of trial." (*Wisdom* 3:18). Make me know now as I shall know then what vanity is, and then how can I ever be arrogant again in the face of that most certain truth? "Vanity of vanities, and all is vanity." (*Eccles.* 1:2). Job was always humble, even in the days of his prosperity: "My days shall be shortened, and only the grave remaineth for me." (*Job* 17:1).

53. Another humiliating thought lies in the remembrance of the Judgment to come. Saints tremble at the thought that they will be judged by a God in whose presence not even the Angels are immaculate. They tremble, although they have nothing for which to be judged, except their good works. And what will become of me, therefore, who am guilty of so many sins?

Therefore, if I esteem myself and seek to be esteemed by others, either as more virtuous or less sinful than I really am, it is certain that such a desire can only arise from my own hypocrisy, by which I appear before the eyes of men under a false disguise, leading them to believe that I am one thing, when I am really another, because I know that they cannot see what is going on in my heart. But a time will come when God will reveal my wickedness to the whole world: "I will show thy nakedness to the nations, and thy shame to kingdoms." (*Nahum* 3:5). And then I shall appear as I really am. And what will they say of me who have been deceived by my false dissemblings?

O my Soul, be humble and forget not that the more thou art exalted in thy own esteem, the more wilt thou be shamed and confounded at the Judgment Day. For then, as the Prophet says,

"Man shall be humbled," (*Is.* 5:15), and only the humble will be able to glory "in his exultation." (*James* 1:9). Remember that according to the saying of Isaias, the Day of Judgment has been appointed especially to humble the proud: "Because the day of the Lord of hosts shall be on every one that is proud and highminded . . . and he shall be humbled," (*Is.* 2:12); and thou shouldst regard as though specially directed to thyself that prophetic voice from God which says: "Behold I come against thee, O proud one, saith the Lord the God of hosts, for thy day is come, the time of thy visitation. And the proud one shall fall; he shall fall down, and there shall be none to lift him up." (*Jeremias* 50:31-32).

Ah, how can I indeed esteem myself more than others when we have all to appear as criminals, miserable and naked, before God's judgment seat? So writes St. Paul in his Epistle to the Romans: "But thou, why judgest thou thy brother? Or thou, why dost thou despise thy brother? For we shall all stand before the judgment seat of Christ." (*Rom.* 14:10).

54. O my Soul, humble thyself in the remembrance that there is a Hell, not considering it only in the abstract, nor even as a contrivance for the punishment of sinners in general, but regard it rather as a place specially prepared for thyself and deserved by thee more than once!

For there the proud will be cast headlong, and I should be there with them at this moment, eternally insulted and tormented by devils, had I not been preserved therefrom by the mercy of God. Millions of angels have been imprisoned there for having committed one sole sin of pride, and that only in thought. Ah, my Soul, continue thus in thy pride and thy false self-esteem, guarding thy own susceptibilities and oblivious to the rights of others, and "thou shalt be brought down to Hell"; that place of torment awaits thee, and there below thy pride shall indeed be humbled. Thou who delightest now in thy own proud thoughts shalt there be thrust into flames of fire, and thou who now wishest to be above all shalt then be below all. For there below thou wilt have to face a God who bears an infinite hatred of the proud and is infinitely angry with them. And as it is a truth that the humble shall be exalted in Heaven, it is also a truth that the proud shall be humbled and cast down into Hell.

"And the rich man also died." Thus writes St. Luke of a proud man who was "clothed in purple and fine linen." And the rich man died—that is the end of all humanity, and vanity. And "he was buried in hell" (*Luke* 16:22)—that is the end of all pride. The grave is the end of man; Hell is the end of the proud.

55. But above all, the thought of eternity should keep us humble. Taking it for granted that I am mistaken in practicing humility in this world and in giving place to others, I know that my mistake is small because everything below comes quickly to an end. But if I am deceiving myself by living in reckless pride, my mistake is great because it will last for all eternity. But even if I am living in humility, I must still fear because I can never be sure whether this humility which I think I possess is true humility or not; how much more, then, should I fear if I am living in open pride? So be it, O my Soul! Satisfy all thy proud desires: be thou esteemed, praised and honored by all the world; possess knowledge, riches and pleasure without adversity, without opposition, without any obstacles to trouble thee or restrain thy vicious passions. And then? And then? I pray thee in this to imitate the proud Nabuchodonosor, who even in the fullness of his power thought of "what should come to pass hereafter." (*Daniel* 2:29). All is vanity that hath an end; and we are doomed to enter into that eternity which hath no end; therefore, what will be the end of the vanity of thy pride? The most ignominious humiliations and most bitter lamentations—that will last forever and ever.

On this side of the grave all things pass away, but on the other side, what will become of me? *Quid futurum post hæc?*—"What future will come after this?" To this I give no thought; and to speak the truth, this is the reason why I am dominated by vanity, because I give so little thought to eternity. King David was most humble of heart because he was filled with the dread of eternity: "And I meditate in the night with my own heart . . . Will God then cast off for ever?" (*Ps.* 76:7-8). Whenever the world offers thee honors, fame and pleasure, remember, my Soul, to say within thy-self: "And then? And then?" "Remember what things have been before thee." (*Ecclus.* 41:5).

How many of those who were conspicuous among the proud of this world have overcome their pride and acquired humility by one single serious thought of eternity! The words of the Prophet have always been and always will be found true: "And the ancient mountains were crushed to pieces, the hills of the world were bowed down by the journeys of His eternity." (*Hab.* 3:6).

56. There is one kind of pride which is more abominable in the eyes of God than any other, and it is that, says Holy Writ, which belongs more especially to the poor. "My soul hateth . . . a poor man that is proud." (*Ecclus.* 25:3-4). If the pride of one who is rich in merit, talents and virtues—treasures most precious to the soul—is displeas-ing to God, still more displeasing to Him will it be in one who has not these same motives for pride, but who on the contrary has every reason to be humble. And this, I fear, is the pride of which I am guilty.

I am poor in soul, without virtue or merit, full of iniquity and malice, and yet I esteem myself and love my own esteem so much that I am trou-bled if others do not esteem me also. I am truly a poor, proud, miserable creature; and the greater my poverty, the more my pride is detestable in the eyes of God. All this proceeds from not knowing myself. Grant, O my God, that I may say with the Prophet: "I am the man that see my poverty." (*Lam.* 3:1). Make known unto me, O Lord, mine own wretchedness, that of myself I am nothing, know nothing, and possess nothing but my sins, and deserve nothing but Hell. I have received from Thee many graces, lights and inspirations, and much help, and yet with what ingratitude have I responded to Thine infinite goodness! Who is more sinful, who more ungrateful, and who more wicked than I? The more Thou hast done for me, the more humble I ought to be, for I shall have to render unto Thee a most strict account of all Thy benefits: "And unto whomsoever much is given, of him much shall be required." (*Luke* 12:48). And yet the greater Thy goodness, the greater my pride. I blush with shame, and it is the knowledge of my pride that obliges me now to be humble.

57. It is easier to be humble in adversity than in prosperity, and it is impossible to say how much temporal happiness influences man to be proud. "They are not in the labor of men." (*Ps.* 72:5). Thus the Prophet-King speaks of sinners, and adds: "Therefore pride hath held them fast." (*Ps.* 72:6).

Adversity counterbalances our self-love and prevents its growth, for on the one hand it makes known our frailties to us, the more so when it is unexpected and grievous; and on the other hand, it compels us to turn our thoughts to God, implore His mercy and humble ourselves under

His hand, as did the Prophet: "In my affliction I called upon the Lord." (*Ps.* 17:7). "And as one sorrowful, so was I humbled." (*Ps.* 34:14). Therefore, if we know not how to bear our tribulations with cheerfulness, let us at least endure them with patience and humility.

Oh, how precious are those humiliations by which we acquire and learn to exercise humility! It is then that we ought to exclaim with the Psalmist, "Thou hast humbled the proud one, as one that is slain," (*Ps.* 88:11), or else like King Nabuchodonosor when he came to his senses and humbly exclaimed, "Therefore I do now praise and magnify and glorify the King of heaven, because . . . them that walk in pride he is able to abase." (*Dan.* 4:34). Afflictions are not wanting in this vale of tears, but there are few who know how to use them as a means of becoming humble. Grant of Thy mercy, O my God, that I may be among those few!

58. We must not be too apt to flatter ourselves that we possess any special virtue. Our chastity may be the result of an absence of opportunities or temptations; and in like manner, our patience may proceed from a phlegmatic temperament, or be dictated by worldly and not by Christian wisdom. This can be said of many other virtues in which we are liable to make the same mistake.

We must study this doctrine well, that the true Christian virtues are "born not of blood, nor of the will of the flesh, nor of the will of man, but of

God," (*John* 1:13), that is, that they are not the work either of the desires, passions or reason of man, but proceed from God as their First Principle and return to God as their Last End. This knowledge is necessary for us, so that we may not imagine ourselves to be virtuous when we are not, nor think ourselves better than others when we see them falling into some sin.

We should ever learn lessons of humility from the faults of others and say: "If I had found myself in like circumstances and had had the same temptation, perhaps I should have done worse. If God does not permit great temptations to assail me, it is because He knows my weakness and that I should succumb to them; with eyes of compassion He sees what I am, 'a weak man.' (*Wisdom* 9:5). And if I do not fall into sin, it is not by my own virtue, but by God's grace. Let me therefore abide in humility, and it is to my advantage, because if in my pride I count myself greater than others, God will abandon me and suffer me to fall and will humble me through those very things for which I wish to exalt myself. Listen to the advice of St. Augustine: "I make bold to say that it is profitable for the proud to fall, in order that they may be humbled in that for which they have exalted themselves." [36]

59. Whenever it happens that we do good to the

---

36. *"Audeo dicere, superbis expedit cadere, ut in eo, in quo se extollunt, humilientur."* (Serm. 53, *de Verb. Dom.*)

souls of others, either by instruction or good advice, or by our discourses and good example, it is then more than at any other time that we should consider ourselves bound to be humble for this reason, which is founded on faith and truth: God chooses things most vile, most weak, most base and most worthy of contempt in this world for the fulfillment of His great purposes, and this is a truth revealed by the Holy Ghost through the mouth of St. Paul: "But the foolish things of the world . . . and the weak things of the world . . . and the base things of the world, and the things that are contemptible, hath God chosen." (*1 Cor.* 1:27-28).

Therefore, it follows that if God has made me His instrument to sow good seed in the souls of others, that they may bring forth fruit unto everlasting life, which is the most wonderful work that proceeds from His mercy and omnipotence, I must in consequence count myself in truth among the vilest and most contemptible things of this world. "And the base things of the world, and the things that are contemptible . . . and things that are not." (*1 Cor.* 28). This is an article of Faith.

If a soul were to be lost through my bad example or advice, I should certainly be the author and cause of its destruction, but if a soul should be saved either by my word or deed, I cannot attribute the glory to myself, because the salvation of that soul will have been wholly the work of God: "Salvation is of the Lord." (*Ps.* 3:9).

The gifts of knowledge, wisdom and eloquence,

and even of working miracles, are graces that are called *gratis datæ*—"freely given"—and are sometimes even given to the wicked. Sanctifying Grace alone, which is given to him who lives in humility and charity, is that which renders the soul precious in the eyes of God, but no one is sure of possessing it.

60. As Paradise is only for the humble, therefore in Paradise everyone will have more or less glory according to his degree of humility. God has exalted Jesus Christ in glory above all, because He was the humblest of all; being the true Son of God, He yet elected to become the most abject of all men. And after Jesus Christ, the most exalted of all was His Holy Mother, because being superior to all in her dignity as Mother of God, yet she humbled herself more than all by her profound humility. This rule, dictated by the wisdom of God, applies to all the other Saints who are exalted in their glory in Heaven in proportion to their humility on earth.

Holy Writ says truly that "Humility goeth before glory." (*Prov.* 15:33). Job had said the same: "For he that hath been humbled shall be in glory." (*Job* 22:29). But the Saviour of the world spoke more plainly still when, having shown that humility is necessary to enter the Kingdom of Heaven, He called unto Him a little child and said: "Whosoever therefore shall humble himself as this little child, he is the greater in the kingdom of heaven." (*Matt.* 18:4). And oh how precious humility must be when God recompenses it with eternal glory! Oh my Soul, lift up the eyes of thy faith to Paradise, and consider whether it be not best to be humble in our short existence here on earth, in order to enter with joy into the immeasurable glory of that happy eternity? "For that which is at present momentary ... worketh for us above measure exceedingly an eternal weight of glory." (*2 Cor.* 4:17). Recommend thyself with all thy heart to that God, "Who setteth up the humble on high." (*Job* 5:11).

61. The proof of true humility is patience: neither meekness of speech, nor humbleness of bearing, nor the giving up of oneself to lowly works, is a sufficient indication by which to judge if a soul is truly humble. There are many who bear all the appearance of exterior humility, but who are angered at every slight adversity and resent any little vexation which they may encounter.

If under certain circumstances we show toleration and patience in bearing an insult, in suffering a wrong in silence without indignation and anger or resentment, it is a good sign, and we may begin to conclude that we have some humility; but even then, patience can only be an infallible sign of true humility when it proceeds from the recognition of our own unworthiness and when we tolerate the wrong because we know that we ourselves are full of faults and are deserving of it.

And how do we stand, O my Soul, in regard to

this patience? O my God, how much pride I find, even in my patience! Sometimes I suffer a wrong, but at the same time I feel that I am wronged. I suffer an insult, but consider that I do not deserve it. And if others do not esteem me, yet I esteem myself. Is there humility here? Not a vestige of it!

The Holy Fathers attribute to Jesus Christ the words which the Prophet says of himself: "For I am ready for scourges," (*Ps.* 37:18), because by reason of our iniquities which He had taken upon Himself, He considered Himself deserving of all the penalties and opprobrium of the world. Here is the pattern of true humility.

Very different is the patience of the philosophers and stoics and the patience of worldly people, from that of true Christians. The stoics taught great patience in their writings and by their example, but it was a patience that was the outcome of pride, self-esteem and contempt for others. The worldly-minded, it is true, bear the many anxieties and afflictions of their own state of life with patience, but it is a patience that proceeds from interested motives, or the necessity of worldly prudence. Christians alone possess that patience united to humility which receives every adversity with submission to the Divine Will, and this is the patience which is pleasing to God. For, as St. Augustine says: "That which a man does from pride is not pleasing to God, but that which he does from humility is acceptable to Him."

62. The following thoughts may sometimes trou-

ble us: Who knows whether my past Confessions
have been good? Who knows whether I have had
real sorrow for my sins? Who knows if my sins
have been forgiven? Who knows whether I am in
the grace of God? Who knows whether I shall
obtain the grace of final perseverance? And who
knows if I am predestined to be saved? But it is
not God's intention that this uncertainty should
cause us these anxieties and scruples. In His infinite wisdom, He has hidden from us the mysteries of His justice and mercy, so that our ignorance
should prove a most efficacious help to keep us in
humility. Therefore, the profit we ought to derive
from such thoughts is this: to live always in fear
and humility before God, to do good diligently,
and to avoid evil without ever exalting ourselves
above others in our self-esteem, because we do not
know what our doom may be. "Serve ye the Lord
with fear." (*Ps.* 2:11). "Fear the Lord, all ye His
saints." (*Ps.* 33:10).

Such is the Divine Will toward us, manifested
through St. Paul. God expects us always to be
humble, whether it be for that which He reveals
to us, or for that which He withholds from us.
When we read the Holy Scriptures, we find many
prophecies proceeding from the Holy Ghost that
terrify us, but many others that console us. When
we read the writings of the Holy Fathers, we find
in them some judgments that are very terrible
and some that are very lenient. When we read the
theological works of the scholastics, we find in
them opinions upon the subjects of grace and pre-

destination that alarm us and others that encourage us. Why is this? The Providence of God has thus disposed it, so that between hope and fear we might remain humble.

The mysteries of grace and predestination would no longer be mysteries if we were capable of grasping them with our understanding. To pause and consider whether God has forgiven our sins or not, and whether we are living in a state of grace, or whether we are predestined, etc., is in itself an act of temerity and pride, inasmuch as we are seeking to know the hidden judgments of God, who does not wish us to know them, so that we may remain in humility. "Be not highminded, but fear," says St. Paul. (*Rom.* 11:20).

63. I ought to be most grateful to anyone who helps to keep me in humility by subjecting me to humiliations of word and deed, because he is cooperating with the divine mercy to fulfill the work of my eternal salvation. And although he has no thought of my salvation when he offends me, he is nevertheless an instrument thereof, and all the evil comes from me if I do not make a good use of it. St. Ambrose says of David when he was insulted by Semei with vituperations and stoning, that he "held his peace and humbled himself," (Lib. 1, *Offic.,* C. 18), keeping his mind fixed on this one thought: "The Lord hath bid him curse me." (*2 Kgs.* 16:10). We are grateful to the surgeon who bleeds us, even though he may not be thinking of our health, but of this particular office of his profession.[37] Therefore, if we understood this, not as Stoic philosophers, but as good Christians, we ought to be grateful to those who humiliate us, for although they have no intention of making us humble, but only of humiliating us, yet in reality this humiliation helps us to acquire humility—if such be our desire.

The benefit is a real benefit, although he who confers it has no intention that it should be so. An insult is only an insult in the intention of the man who gives it, and the humiliation belongs only to him who receives it; and it is a most sure means of acquiring and practicing humility, if he knows how to receive it in a Christian spirit.

To this end, God permits us to be humiliated at times, so that we may give a proof of our virtue "in the furnace of humiliation," (*Ecclus.* 2:5), and the teacher of this wise rule goes on to say: "Humble thy heart and endure." (*Ecclus.* 2:2).

64. Everything depends upon the way in which we take things. To rule our life by the maxims of the world is certain to inspire pride, and it is equally certain that to rule ourselves by the maxims of the Gospel will inspire humility. According to the world, we should repulse an insult with anger and resentment; but according to the Gospel, we should accept it with a humble, pru-

---

37. The reader should remember that this book first appeared before 1753, when "bleeding" a patient was still considered an acceptable medical practice, which today it obviously is not.—*Publisher*, 2006.

dent and meek patience. "This saying is hard." (*John* 6:61). But how much patience do we not exercise to please the world—patience that is often bitter and hard! And shall it therefore be a "hard saying" that we are to have patience and humility in order to please God? Ah, miserable Soul of mine, let us attach to the things of this world the thoughts and ideas and scruples of this world—its obligations and opinions, its politics and loves and caprices! I know well that humility can only be laborious and wearisome in such an atmosphere, so full of worldliness, for as Holy Writ says: "Humility is an abomination to the proud." (*Ecclus.* 13:24). But let us rise above the world and its opinions, and in the light of the eternal truth of faith, we shall find that this virtue is not only easy, but sweet and pleasing, because all that Christ has told us is true. And after having exhorted us to learn humility from Him, "Learn of Me for I am meek and humble of heart," (*Matt.* 11:29), He immediately added, "For My yoke is sweet and My burden light." (*Matt.* 11:30). Truth cannot lie; it is we who refuse to listen to it. We are ruled by the world, and so to hear humility spoken of is a "hard saying." But let us remember that it is a "true saying." For if we are not humble, we cannot be saved.

Great is the kingdom to which we aspire, says St. Augustine, but humble is the way which leads to it: *Excelsa est patria, humilis est via.* [Literally, "Great is the Fatherland; humble is the way."] Of what use is our longing for Paradise if we will not walk in the path of humility, which is the only way that leads to it? "Why does he seek his native land who refuses to follow the way that leads to it?"[38]

65. When I consider the words which Jesus Christ addressed to His heavenly Father in prayer, saying that He did not pray for the world—"I pray not for the world" (*John* 17:9)— and again that, when praying for His disciples, that His prayer might be more efficacious, He emphasized the fact that they were not followers of the world—"These are in the world . . . but they are not of the world" (*John* 17:11, 16)—I confess that no words of our Saviour in the whole Gospel terrify me more than these. For I perceive that it is necessary for me to separate myself from the world, so that Jesus Christ may intercede for me. And if I am a lover of the world, I shall be excommunicated by Jesus Christ and shall have no part in His intercessions and prayers. These are the words of Christ Himself: "I pray not for the world, but for . . . those who are not of the world." (*John* 17:9 ff.)

Let us really understand these words: that Jesus Christ excludes us from His kingdom if we belong to the world, that is to say, if we wish to follow the maxims of the world, which are nothing but vanity and deceit and fill man with pride— the maxims of the world, which the Prophet says, "Turn aside the way of the humble." (*Amos* 2:7).

---

38. *"Qui recusat viam, quid quærit patriam?"* (Tract. 78).

Meanwhile, Jesus Christ is our advocate with the Father in so far as, renewing our Baptismal vows, we renounce the world and accept the maxims of the Gospel, which are true and tend to make man humble. To serve both God and the world is impossible, because we could never please both— "He will hold to the one and despise the other." (*Luke* 16:13).

To pretend to serve God and the world is the same as to imagine that we can be both humble and proud at the same time. A vain dream!

66. The most familiar meditation which the seraphic St. Francis was in the habit of making was this: First he elevated his thoughts to God and then turned them toward himself: "My God," he would exclaim, "Who art Thou, and who am I?" And raising his thoughts first to the greatness and infinite goodness of God, he would then descend to consider his own misery and vileness. And thus ascending and descending this scale of thought from the greatness of God down to his own nothingness, the Seraphic Saint would pass whole nights in meditation, practicing in this exercise a real, true, sublime and profound humility, like the Angels on that ladder of mystical perfection, ascending and descending by it, seen by Jacob in his sleep. (*Gen.* 28:12).

This should be our model, that we may not err in the exercise of humility. To fix our thoughts solely on our own wretchedness might cause us to fall into self-distrust and despair, and in the same way to fix our thoughts solely on the contemplation of the Divine Goodness might cause us to be presumptuous and rash. True humility lies between the two: "Humility," says St. Thomas, "checks presumption and strengthens the soul against despair."[39]

Distrust yourself and confide in God, and thus distrusting and thus confiding, between fear and hope, you shall work out your salvation in the spirit of the Gospel.

We should first reflect upon the infinite mercy of God, in order to excite our hope, as King David did: "Thy mercy is before my eyes." And then we should reflect on His justice, in order to keep ourselves in the fear thereof: "O Lord, I will be mindful of Thy justice alone." (*Ps.* 70:16). And also, in turning our thoughts to ourselves, we should first reflect upon man as being the work of God, created to His image and likeness, in order to give God the glory; then we should reflect upon the sinner in man, which is our work and which ought to make us deeply dejected. "Man and sin," says St. Augustine, "are as it were two distinct things. What savors of man, God made; what savors of the sinner, man made himself. Destroy what man has made, that God may save what He has made."[40]

---

39. *"Humilitas præsumtionem et firmat animum contra desperationem"* (IIa IIæ, Q. 161, art. 1).
40. *"Quasi duæ res sunt homo et peccator. Quod audis homo; Deus fecit; quod audis peccator ipse homo fecit. Dele quod fecisti ut Deus salvet quod fecit."* (Tract. 12, in 10).

67. Self-knowledge is a great help for acquiring humility; but in the midst of the many passions, faults and vices of which we are aware, to recognize our own pride is the most useful of all. For this vice is the most shameful of all. And even in our Confessions, it is more difficult for us to say truthfully: "I accuse myself of being proud and of not trying seriously to correct this fault," than to accuse ourselves of many other sins. This knowledge of our pride is most humiliating; for where certain other vices may be pitied and excused for some reason or other, pride can never be pitied or excused, being a sin which is diabolical and odious, not only to God, but to men—as the Inspired Word says: "Pride is hateful before God and men." (*Ecclus.* 10:7).

Let us therefore examine ourselves daily on this point; let us accuse ourselves of it in our Confessions, and acknowledging our pride in this manner will be an excellent incentive to become humble. Let us pray to Jesus Christ that He may do for us as He did for the blind man whom He healed, and ask Him to put the mud of pride upon our eyes so that we may be made to see. Let us say to God: "Thou art my God, that God who 'raiseth up the needy from the earth and lifteth up the poor out of the dunghill,' (*Ps.* 112:7), grant that this pride which is my great sin may through Thee serve as an instrument by which I may attain to a virtuous humility!"

68. Let us consider the things of this world in

which we are apt to take a vain delight. One may pride himself on his robust health and bodily strength; another on the science, knowledge, eloquence and other gifts that he has acquired through study and art. Another prides himself upon his wealth and possessions; another upon his nobility and rank; another upon his moral virtues, or other virtues which bring him spiritual grace and perfection. But must not all these gifts be regarded as so many benefits proceeding from God, for which we must render an account if we do not use them to resist temptation and conform to the ordination of God? We are debtors to God for every benefit that we receive and are bound to employ these gifts and to trade with them for the glory of God, like merchants to whom capital is entrusted. When we consider how many benefits, both of body and soul, we have received from Him, we are compelled to admit that there are so many debts which we have contracted toward Him— and why should we glory in our debts?

No prudent merchant, if he has large debts, would go and proclaim the fact in the marketplace and thereby lose his credit; and how can we expect to gain credit by boasting of the many debts we owe to God—debts so heavy that we run the risk of becoming bankrupt on that day when Our Lord and Master will say: "Pay what thou owest." (*Matt.* 8:28).

From the benefits we receive of God, we should learn lessons of humility, rather than of pride, following the teaching of St. Gregory: "The more strict the account that a man sees he must give of his duties, the more humble should he be in the performance of them."[41] Our desire to boast of the favors we have received of God only demonstrates our ingratitude, and we have more cause to humble ourselves for being ungrateful than to glory in the benefits thus bestowed upon us.

69. The true reason for which God bestows so many graces upon the humble is this, that the humble are faithful to these graces and make good use of them. They receive them from God and use them in a manner pleasing to God, giving all the glory to Him, without reserving any for themselves.

This is like the faithful steward who appropriates nothing that belongs to his master; and thus deserves that praise and reward given to the faithful servant mentioned in the Gospel: "Well done, thou good and faithful servant; because thou hast been faithful over a few things, I will place thee over many things." (*Matt.* 25:21).

O my Soul, how dost thou stand in regard to this faithfulness toward God? Art thou not like those servants to whom their master daily entrusts money now to buy one thing, now another, and who each time keep back a small coin for themselves, until little by little they

---

41. "*Tanto ergo esse humilior quisque debet eo munere, quanto se obligatiorem esse conspicit in reddenda ratione.*" (Hom. 9, *in Evang.*).

become unfaithful servants and great thieves? In like manner, our pride renders us unfaithful servants when we attribute to ourselves that praise which is due only to a gift that is entrusted to us by God and which ought to be ascribed unreservedly to Him.

O Lord, Thou seest all my thefts, and I am overwhelmed with astonishment that Thou dost still trust me! Considering my unfaithfulness, I am not worthy of the smallest grace; but make me humble, and I shall also be faithful.

It is certainly true that he who is humble is also faithful to God, because the humble man is also just in giving to all their due, and above all, in rendering to God the things that are God's; that is, in giving Him the glory for all the good that he is, all the good that he has and for all the good that he does; as the Venerable Bede says: "Whatever good we see in ourselves, let us ascribe it to God and not to ourselves." [42]

70. To give thanks to God for all the blessings we have received and are continually receiving is an excellent means of exercising humility, because by thanksgiving we learn to acknowledge the Supreme Giver of every good. And for this reason it is necessary for us always to be humble before God. St. Paul exhorts us to render thanks for all things and at all times: "In all things give

---

42. *"Ut si quid nobis boni inesse deprehendimus, non nobis sed Deo adscribamus."* (*Apud* D. Th. *in Cat.* to 5).

thanks." (*1 Thess.* 5:18). "Giving thanks always for all things." (*Eph.* 5:20). But that our thanksgiving may be an act of humility it must not only come from the lips but from the heart, with a firm conviction that all good comes to us through the infinite mercy of God. Look at a beggar who has received a considerable gift from a rich man, with what warmth he expresses his gratitude! He is astonished that the rich man should have deigned to bestow a gift upon him, protesting that he is unworthy of it and that he receives it, not through his own merit, but through the noble kindness of the giver, to whom he will always be most grateful. He speaks from his heart because he knows his own miserable condition of poverty and the benign condescension of the rich man. And should the thanks we give to God be less than the thanks which are given from man to man? When one man can thus thank another, ought we not to blush with shame that there should be men who feel more humility of heart toward their fellow-men than we do toward God?

O my God, I thank Thee with all my heart for these benefits which I have received through Thy goodness alone, which I have not deserved and for which I have never given Thee thanks till now! It was through pride that I failed to give Thee the thanks due to Thee, and it is through pride that I have enjoyed all Thy gifts as if I had not received them at Thy hands. I detest my pride, and with Thy help, I will remember to give Thee thanks at all times and for all things: "I will bless the Lord at all times," (*Ps.* 33:1), praise, bless and thank Thee for all Thy mercies forever and ever: "The mercies of the Lord I will sing for ever." (*Ps.* 88:1).

71. The important point is that our heart should be humble, because this is what Christ seeks in us above all things. It is useless to mend the case and hands of a watch, unless we also adjust the wheels and the works. And in the same way, it is useless for anyone to be modest in attire and bearing, if there be no true humility in the heart.

We ought to apply our Saviour's sayings to ourselves: "Thou blind Pharisee, first make clean the inside of the cup and of the dish, that the outside may become clean," (*Matt.* 23:26), and learn from the teaching of St. Thomas that "from our interior disposition of humility proceed signs in words, deed and manner by which that is manifested without, which is within."[43]

I admit the truth of that which was so often repeated in Holy Writ, that humility is a special gift of God and that no one can possess it of himself, "except God gave it." (*Wis.* 8:21). But at the tribunal of God there will be no excuse for us for not having possessed humility, because we have been taught that we could obtain it by persevering prayer; and if we have not used this means to obtain it, it will be our fault that we have not

---

43. "*Ex interiore dispositione humilitatis procedunt signa in verbis et factis et gestibus, quibus id, quod interius latet, manifestatur.*" (IIa IIæ, Q. 161, art. 6).

asked God for it and therefore our fault that we have not obtained it.

Our Saviour in His Gospel says: "Ask and you shall receive." (*John* 16:24). If you want anything of Me, ask and you shall be heard. And can this virtue cost us less than the simple effort of asking it of God with great insistence? Therefore, let us not cease to ask for it; and by the very method of obtaining it, our hearts, our looks, our words, our movements, our bearing, and even our very thoughts will all be humble: "For from the heart come forth . . . thoughts." (*Matt.* 15:19).

72. We often lament that we are unable to pray because of the many distractions which hinder our recollection and dry up the source of devotion in our hearts, but in this we err and do not know what we are saying. The best prayer is not that in which we are most recollected and fervent, but that in which we are most humble, because it is written: "The prayer of him that humbleth himself shall pierce the clouds." (*Ecclus.* 35:21). And what distractions of mind and heart can prevent our exercising humility?

It is precisely in those moments when we feel irritable and tepid that we ought to show our humility, and how? By saying: "O Lord, I am not worthy to remain here speaking to Thee so confidentially; I do not deserve the grace of prayer because it is a special gift which Thou bestowest upon those dear to Thee. It is enough for me to be Thy servant, chasing away my distractions as so many flies. For flies do not fly round boiling water, but only round tepid water, and all these distractions arise from my great tepidity." Ah, what an excellent prayer! So prayed Josias, and the Lord heard his prayer: "Thou hast humbled thyself in the sight of God . . . I also have heard thee, saith the Lord." (*2 Par.* 34:27). So prayed King David too in the anguish of his soul and was delivered: "I was humbled, and He delivered me." (*Ps.* 114:6). The more the soul exalts itself and takes pleasure in its own meditation, so much the more does God exalt Himself above that soul and remains apart from it. "Man shall come to a deep heart, and God shall be exalted." (*Ps.* 63:7-8). Do we desire that God in His mercy should come nigh to us? Let us humble ourselves. "Dost thou wish God to draw near to thee?" says St. Augustine; "Humble thyself, for the more thou raisest thyself, the more will He be above thee."[44]

73. Many people, when preparing for Confession, distress themselves because they do not feel sufficient contrition for their sins; and in order to obtain it, they beat their breasts to try to excite themselves to feelings of sorrow. But this is pride, for they give us to understand that they can thus obtain contrition of themselves. You desire true sorrow for your sins? Then be assured that this is a singular gift of God, and that to obtain it, there

---

44. *"Vis tibi propinquet Deus? Humilia te; nam tanto a te erit altior quanto tu elatior."* (Enarr. in *Ps.* 141).

is no better means than to humble oneself before Him.

Humility generates confidence, and God never refuses His grace to those who come to Him with humility and trust. Say therefore to God: "I can remain here as long as I like and do all that I can to obtain sorrow for my sins, but it is impossible for me to attain to it of myself, if Thou dost not grant it to me, O my God! I do not deserve it, but Jesus Christ has merited it for me, and it is through His merits that I ask it, and through Thine infinite goodness that I hope to obtain it."

Place yourself in this humble disposition of mind and you will be happy, for it is written of God that He "comforteth the humble," (*2 Cor.* 7:6), and "He hath had regard to the prayer of the humble, and he hath not despised their petition." (*Ps.* 101:18). This sorrow or contrition by which the soul is sanctified is one of the greatest graces that God can give us, and it would be presumption, temerity, and pride on our part to pretend to this grace without having asked for it with due humility.

74. A doubt may arise in our mind—that, since to obtain the grace of humility, we must ask it of God, and ask it with humility if we wish God to hear our prayer—how can we possibly ask with humility, since it is precisely that humility which we have not and for which we are asking? Let us not lose ourselves in such speculations, which are useless in practice, since simplicity of heart is what the Lord desires of us. (*Wis.* 1:1).

There are certain efficacious virtues that God has infused into our souls in holy Baptism, independently of our own dispositions, "principally by infusion in Baptism," says St. Thomas. Such, for example, is faith, and such also is that humility which is necessary for us, so that we may believe and pray as we ought. Let us therefore exercise in our prayers this infused humility; and in making good use of it, we shall in time acquire that other evangelical virtue which is necessary to our salvation and which can only be obtained by our own co-operation.

Prayer, says St. Augustine, is essentially the resource of him who knows that he is both poor and needy: "Prayer is only for the needy."[45] Let us acknowledge and confess our poverty and indigence before God, and by this confession we shall exercise humility. The really poor do not need to be taught how to ask alms humbly. Necessity is their master, and if man can humble himself before man, why should he not also humble himself before God?

If we wish to discern what belongs to God and that which is our own, it is sufficient for us to reflect that by rendering to God all that is His, nothing is left to ourselves but nothingness, so that we can truly say with the Prophet: "I am brought to nothing." (*Ps.* 72:21). This is a true saying, that all that is within us that is more than nothingness belongs to God, and He can take

---

45. *"Oratio non est nisi indigentium."* (Enarr. in *Ps.* 26).

away what is His when He chooses, without doing us any wrong. Therefore, in what can we pride ourselves, since God can take anything away from us the moment that we begin to glory in it?

For he who glories in his wealth may soon become poor; he who glories in his health may suddenly become infirm; he who glories in his knowledge may suddenly become insane; he who glories in his holiness may suddenly fall into some great sin. What vanity, what folly, then, to glory in that which is not our own, nor even in our power to keep! "What hast thou that thou hast not received?" (*1 Cor.* 4:7).

This reflection alone should suffice to make us humble, and it may be said that all true humility depends upon our persevering seriously in this thought. Oh, my Soul, thou shalt be humbled when, as God says by the Prophet, He will "separate the precious from the vile." (*Jer.* 15:19). Thus the essence of humility consists in knowing how to discern rightly that which is mine and that which belongs to God. All the good I do comes from God, and nothing belongs to me but my own nothingness. What was I in the abyss of eternity? A mere nothing. And what did I do of myself to emerge from that nothingness? Nothing. If God had not created me, where should I be? In nothingness. If God did not uphold me at every turn, whither should I return? Into nothingness. Therefore, it is clear that I possess nothing *of myself* but nothingness. Even in my moral being, I possess nothing but my own wickedness. When I do evil, it is entirely my own work; when I do good, it belongs to God alone.[46] Evil is a work of my own wickedness; good is a work of God's mercy. In this way we separate the precious from the vile; this is the art of all arts, the science of sciences and the wisdom of the Saints.

76. Let us imagine a man who possesses many beasts of burden, which he has bought for the purpose of carrying such loads as he requires. The beasts are loaded, one with gold, one with books of philosophy, mathematics, theology and law, another with weapons, another with sacred vessels and vestments belonging to the Church, and another with reliquaries in which are precious relics of the Saints, and so on.

Now, if these animals could discourse among themselves, do you think that the one laden with gold would boast of his riches, and the one laden

---

46. This statement is not intended to deny the fact that a person in the state of grace is actually a *doer* of the good works that he performs. As the Council of Trent states, "If anyone says that the good works of the one justified are in such manner the gifts of God that they are not also the good merits of him justified . . . let him be anathema." (Sixth Session, Canon 32). Here the author is simply stating, in a dramatic manner, the fact that even man's contribution to his good works is meritorious only by God's grace—by *actual grace* (in so far as this assist from God prompts the person to do the good work), but especially by *Sanctifying Grace,* a gratuitous gift from God through Baptism. For if the person is not in the state of (Sanctifying) grace, his works have no supernatural *merit,* but are only works of natural goodness when that person is in the state of mortal sin). —*Publisher*, 2006.

with books of his knowledge, and that in the same way the others would boast of bravery or of holiness according to the nature of their loads? Would not such pretensions be vain and ridiculous? Most certainly, for the rich and precious burdens borne by these animals belong to the master and not to the beast. For the master might have laden with dung the one he loaded with gold or other precious things; and being their owner, he could unload each animal whenever he pleased, so that each one would appear before him as he is, namely, a vile beast of burden. Or, with St. Augustine, let us picture to ourselves the ass on which Jesus Christ sat when He was met by the multitude with their branches of palms, acclaiming Him with cries of: "Hosanna to the Son of David. . . . Hosanna!" (*Matt.* 21:9). Who would be so foolish as to imagine that these honors were given to the beast? These praises were not given to the ass, but to Christ, who was seated on the ass. "Was that ass to be praised? That ass was carrying someone, but He who was being carried was the one who was being praised."[47]

Let us apply the simile to ourselves, saying with David: "I am become as a beast before thee." (*Ps.* 72:23). And whatever may be the object of our pride, let us use this simile to exercise ourselves in humility.

---

47. *"Laudabatur jumentum illud? Nunquid jumento dicebatur hosanna? Asellus portabat; sed ille qui portabatur, laudabatur."* (*Enarr. in Ps.* 33).

77. We may say with St. Thomas[48] that this craving of ours to be esteemed, respected and honored is an effect of Original Sin, like concupiscence, which remains to us even after our Baptism; but God has ordained that these appetites and desires should remain in us in order that we might have occasion to mortify ourselves and that by such means we might gain the Kingdom of Heaven.

We need not be astonished nor sad when we feel these instincts within us. They belong to the wickedness of our corrupt nature and are remnants of the temptation of our first parents by the Serpent, when he said to them: "And you shall be as gods." (*Gen.* 3:5). Therefore, I repeat that these desires which arise from the weakness and depravity of our human nature must be borne with patience. If these desires gain the mastery over us, it is because we have encouraged and given way to them; and a bad habit which we have formed ourselves can only be cured by ourselves; and therefore the mortification of the same also lies with us. This mortification of the senses, inspired by humility, is taught by Christ in the self-denial which He imposed upon us when He said: "If any man will come after me, let him deny himself." (*Matt.* 16:24). And therefore I must draw this conclusion, that if I will not mortify myself with humility—that is to say, crush my self-love and craving for esteem—I shall be excluded as a follower of Jesus Christ, and by such an exclusion,

---

48. (12, Q. 4, art. 2).

I shall also forfeit His grace and be eternally exiled from participating in His glory.

But in order to practice it, it is necessary for me to do violence to myself, as it is written: "The kingdom of heaven suffereth violence, and the violent bear it away." (*Matt.* 11:12). Who can obtain salvation, except by doing violence to himself?

78. Let us listen at the gates of Hell and hear the lamentations of the eternally damned. They exclaim: "What hath pride profited us?" (*Wis.* 5:8). What use or advantage was our pride to us? Everything passes and vanishes like a shadow, and of all those past evils nothing remains to us but the eternal shame of having been proud.

Their remorse is vain, because it is the remorse of despair. Therefore, while there is still time, let us consider the matter seriously and say: "What advantage have I derived from all my pride? It makes me hateful to Heaven and earth, and if I do not insist upon mortifying it, it will make me odious to myself for all eternity in Hell." Let us lift up our eyes to Heaven and, contemplating the Saints, exclaim: "Behold how their humility has profited them! Oh, how much glory have they gained by their humility!" Now humility is looked upon as madness by the worldly—worthy only of scorn and derision. But a time will come when they will be obliged to recognize its virtue and to exclaim, in seeing the glory of the humble: "Behold how they are numbered among the children of God." (*Wis.* 5:5).

If I am humble, I shall be exalted with that glory to which God exalts the humble. O my God, humble this mad pride which predominates within me. "Thou shalt multiply strength in my soul," (*Ps.* 137:3), for "my strength hath left me." (*Ps.* 37:11). And I will not and cannot do anything without Thy help. In Thee I place all my trust and beseech Thee to help me. "But I am needy and poor; O God, help me. Thou art my helper and my deliverer: O Lord, make no delay." (*Ps.* 69:6).

79. Truly, no one cares to be thought proud, for even according to worldly ideas, the greatest blame that one can give to a man is to say that he is proud. And yet few try to avoid the very thing they would least desire to be accused of by others.

If we feel inward satisfaction when we are given credit for a humility which we do not possess, why do we not endeavor to acquire that with which we like to be credited? If we seek after the vain shadow of humility, it means that we care very little for the substance of this virtue. A man who would be contented with the appearance of virtue, without trying to acquire it in reality, would resemble a merchant who valued false pearls and gems more than real ones.

O my Soul, perhaps thou too art among those who, being proud, resent the accusation of pride and desire to be thought humble! This would be lying to thy own conscience, lying to God, to His Angels and to men. As St. Paul says: "We are made a spectacle to the world, and to angels, and to men." (*1 Cor.* 4:9).

It is a shameful thing for us to wish to appear humble when we are not so. There are certain occasions when in our interior acts we must practice humility; but we must watch over ourselves carefully, so that in thus practicing it, we may not desire to be thought humble. And that is why hidden acts of humility are safer than exterior ones. But if there is pride in wishing that the humility we have should be recognized and known, what measure of presumption would there not be in wishing to be thought humble when we have no humility? Let us beware lest the words of Holy Writ be applicable to ourselves: "There is one that humbleth himself wickedly, and his interior is full of deceit." (*Ecclus.* 19:23).

80. The more we reflect upon this great virtue of humility, the more we should learn to love and honor it. It is natural to the soul to love a good which it recognizes as such, and there is no doubt that we shall love humility when we recognize its intrinsic value and the good that comes of it. Our love of what is good is measured by our knowledge of it, and in the same measure that we love, we desire to obtain it; and in the measure that we desire it, we embrace the most proper and efficacious means of acquiring it. It was thus that the Wise Man [Solomon] acted in order to obtain wisdom. He loved her, desired and prayed for her, and applied his whole mind to possess her, so great was the esteem in which he held her: "Wherefore I wished, and understanding was given me . . . and I preferred her before kingdoms and thrones, and esteemed riches nothing in comparison of her." (*Wis.* 7:7-8).

It is necessary to understand thoroughly this doctrine because we shall never succeed in acquiring humility unless we really desire to obtain it; nor shall we ever desire it unless we have learned to love it; nor shall we love it unless we have realized what humility really is—a great and most precious good, absolutely essential to our eternal welfare. Consider for a little while in what esteem you hold humility. Do you love it? Do you desire it? What do you do to acquire it? Do you ask this virtue of God in your prayers? Do you have recourse to the intercession of the Blessed Virgin? Do you willingly read those books that treat of humility, or the lives of those Saints who were most noted for their humility? "There is a certain will," says St. Thomas, "which had better be called the wish to will than the absolute will itself,"[49] by which it seems that we can will a thing and yet not will it. Therefore, examine yourself and see whether your desire for humility be only a passing velleity [half-hearted will], or really in your will.

---

49. *"Magis est dicenda velleitas quam absoluta voluntas."* (*S.T.*, IIIa, Q. 21, art. 4).

81. To be humble, we must know ourselves, and this self-knowledge is difficult, but only by reason of our pride—the principal effect of which is to blind us. Therefore, to acquire the virtue of humility, we must first fight against and subdue its enemy, pride; and in order to overcome it—having prayed to God with the valiant Judith: "Bring to pass, O Lord, that his pride may be cut off" (*Judith* 9:12)—three other things are necessary.

Firstly, in meditating on the subject, we ought to feel hatred for and abhorrence of our pride, because we can never get rid of all the ills that affect our soul so long as we continue to love them. *Secondly*, we must make a firm resolution of amendment at all cost, because in whatever light we consider it, it will always be to our advantage. *Thirdly*, we should at once endeavor to uproot all our habits of pride, especially those which are most predominant, for it is well known that the longer we allow a bad habit to grow, the stronger it will become, and the greater will be our difficulty in eradicating it: "And I said, now have I begun." (*Ps.* 76:11).

We must not lose heart or be discouraged, but commend ourselves to God's mercy, this being above all things most necessary: "And he will do it." (*Ps.* 36:5). It is through God's grace alone that we can overcome our numerous evil passions, and it is through Him alone that we can hope to subdue our pride. Let us therefore cry unto Him with King David: "My mercy and my refuge: my support and my deliverer: my protector, and I have hoped in him: who subdueth my people under me." (*Ps.* 143:2).

82. Is it not well to apply ourselves to eradicate a fault when we know that by so doing our hearts will be gladdened? And therefore, is it not true that once our pride, which is the cause of so many of our troubles, is subdued, we shall be far happier?

We feel a natural aversion toward the proud, and we cannot love them; but may not this instinct of aversion which we have toward the proud be felt by others toward ourselves? For it is true that "Pride is hateful before God and men." (*Ecclus.* 10:7). Sometimes we lament that others do not love or esteem us. Let us examine the cause, and we shall find that it proceeds from our pride. On the other hand, do we not see the affection that is generally shown toward the humble? Everyone seeks their company, everyone places confidence in them, everyone wishes them well. This would be the case with us if we were humble, and what happiness we should feel in loving and being loved by all! It seems at first as if this were a question of human respect, but it is inspired by charity and comes from God and from a desire to resemble Him. Humility is clad in the same garb as charity, which, St. Paul says, "is patient, is kind, envieth not, is not puffed up, is not ambitious." (*1 Cor.* 13:4). And it is easy to invest humility with the same virtuous intentions as charity.

83. Pride is the root of all our vices, so that when once we have uprooted it, those vices will little by little disappear also. This is the true reason for our having to accuse ourselves of the same sins over and over again in our Confessions, because we never confess that pride which is the root of them all. We do not wonder when we see the fig tree bearing its figs year after year, and the apple tree its apples. No, because each tree bears its own fruit. In the same way, pride is rooted like a tree in our hearts; and our sins of anger, envy, hatred, malice and uncharitableness and rash judgments of others, which we confess over and over again, are the fruit of pride. But as we never strike at the root of this pride, these same sins, like clipped branches, ever sprout out anew. Let us endeavor to eradicate pride thoroughly, following the advice of St. Bernard: "Put the axe to the root,"[50] and then we shall have great joy and consolation in our own conscience.

We must regard pride as the king of all vices and follow the wise advice given by the King of Syria to his captains: "You shall not fight against any, small or great, but against the king of Israel only." (*3 Kgs.* 22:31). Judith too, by killing the proud Holofernes, conquered the whole Assyrian army. And David triumphed over all the Philistines by slaying the proud Goliath. And in like manner we shall also triumph because, by

---

50. *"Securim ponito ad radicem."* (Serm. 2 *de Assump.*).

conquering pride, we shall have subdued all other vices.

King David erred in one thing, for knowing Absalom to be the chief of the rebels, he yet commanded that he should neither be killed nor hurt: "Save me the boy Absalom." (*2 Kgs.* 18:12). Alas, how many imitators he has found! We know full well that pride is the chief rebel among all our passions, but notwithstanding, it is the one which we seem to respect the most and which we almost fear to offend, displaying even a tendency to encourage it.

84. There are certain sins we seldom or never mention in our Confessions, either because our conscience is too easy and elastic or perhaps because we do not really desire to amend. Pride is one of these sins. There are but few who accuse themselves of it, but those who really wish to amend their lives should make it a special subject of their examen and Confession, in order to learn to hate it and repent of it and to make firm resolutions of amendment in the future.

Whoever desires to make a good Confession should not only confess his sin, but also the reason and occasion of the sin, saying for example, "I accuse myself of having taken pleasure in impure thoughts, caused by my want of custody of the eyes, too great freedom of speech and frivolous behavior." And in the same way, we must confess our sins of pride, saying: "I accuse myself of having been angry and annoyed with those around me, and the sole reason of my anger and annoyance was my pride. I accuse myself of having envied and even of having taken what belonged to others, only to satisfy my pride and vanity. I have also spoken with contempt of my neighbor, and this again because of my pride, that can bear no one to be thought superior to myself." Continue to examine all your faults in the same way, and you will find the truth of the inspired words: "The spirit is lifted up before a fall," (*Prov.* 16:18), and "Before destruction the heart of man is exalted." (*Prov.* 18:12).

To subdue our pride, it is well to mortify and shame it by these accusations, which are also acts of virtuous humility; but it is most necessary too to insist upon our own amendment, for "What doth his humbling himself profit him that doth the same again?" (*Ecclus.* 34:31).

It is not enough to confess our sins, Holy Writ says, but it is necessary also to amend them in order to obtain God's mercy: "He that shall confess (his sins) and forsake them shall obtain mercy." (*Prov.* 28:13).

85. Humility of heart, St. Thomas teaches, has no limit, because before God we can always abase ourselves more and more, even unto utter nothingness, and we can do the same to our fellow men; but in the exercise of these exterior acts of humility, it is necessary to be directed with discretion, in order not to fall into an extravagance that might seem excessive. "Humility," says

St. Thomas, "lies chiefly in the soul, and therefore
a man may submit himself to another as regards
his interior acts. And this is what St. Augustine
means when he says: 'Before God a prelate is
placed under your feet, but in exterior acts of
humility, it is necessary to observe due
restraint.'"[51]

Profound humility should exist in every state of
life, but exterior acts of humility are not expedi-
ent to all. For this reason, Holy Writ says:
"Beware that thou be not deceived into folly, and
be humbled." (*Ecclus.* 13:10).

To practice humility of heart in the midst of
pomp and honors, we can learn from the pious
Esther, how she cried to God, "Thou knowest my
necessity, that I abominate the sign of my pride."
(*Esther* 14:16). I attire myself in this rich apparel
and with these jewels because my position
demands it; but Thou, Lord, seest my heart, that
through Thy grace I am not attached to these
things, nor to this apparel, and that I only wear
them of necessity. Here indeed is a great example
of that true inward humility which can be practiced and felt amid external grandeur. But now
we come to the point. This humility of heart must
really exist before God, whose eyes behold the
most hidden motions of the heart; and if it does

---

51. *Humilitas præcipue in anima consistit; et ideo potest homo
secundum interiorem actum alteri se subjicere; et hoc est
quod Augustinus dicit: Coram Deo prælatus substratus sit
pedibus vestris, sed in exterioribus humilitatis actibus est
debita moderatio adhibenda."* (IIa IIæ, Q. 161, art. 3 ad 3).

not exist, what excuse can we allege before the tribunal of God to justify ourselves for not having had it? And the more easily we could have acquired it now, the more inexcusable will it be for us on that day.

86. In reality, the malice of pride lies in the practical contempt which we show for God's Will by disobeying it. Thus it is, says St. Augustine, there is pride in every sin committed, "by which we despise the commandments of God."[52] And St. Bernard explains it in this way, that God commands us to do His Will: "God wishes His Will to be done."[53] And the sinner in his pride prefers his own will to the Will of God: "And the proud man wishes his own will to be done."[54]

And it is this pride that so greatly augments the grievousness of sin; and how great our sin must be when, knowing in our minds that God deserves to be obeyed by us, we oppose our will to the Will of God, whom we know to be worthy of all obedience. What wickedness there is in saying to God, "I will not serve," (*Jer.* 2:20), when we know that all things serve Him. (Cf. *Ps.* 118:91). To give an example of this, let us imagine a person endowed with the noblest qualities possible, such as health, beauty, riches and nobility, and with every natural gift and grace of body and soul.

---

52. *"Qua Dei præcepta contemnimus."* (*Lib. de Salut. docum.* c. 19).
53. *"Vult Deus suam voluntatem fieri."*
54. *"Et superbus vult fieri suam."* (*Serm. 4 in vig. Nat. Dom.*).

Now, little by little, let us take away from that person all those gifts which come from God. Health and beauty are gifts from God; riches and rank, learning and knowledge, and every other virtue are all from God; body and soul belong to God. And this being so, what remains to this person of his own? Nothing, because all that is more than nothing belongs to God.

But when this person says of himself, "I have riches, I have health and I have knowledge," etc., what is meant by this "I"? Nothingness. And yet this "I," this nothingness, that derives all it possesses from God, dares to disregard this same God by disobeying His sovereign commandments, saying to Him (if not in words, most certainly in deeds, which is far worse): "I will not serve! No, I will not obey!" Oh, pride, pride! But, O my Soul, obey! "Why doth thy spirit swell against God?" (*Job* 15:13). Am I not right in preaching and recommending this humility to thee? Each time thou sinnest, thou art like the proud Pharao who said—when he was told to obey the commandments of God—"Who is the Lord . . . I know not." (*Ex.* 5:2).

87. The mistake lies in our having too high an opinion of what the world calls honor, esteem and fame. For however much the world may praise or honor me, it cannot increase my merit or my virtue one jot; and also, if the world vituperates me, it cannot take from me anything that I have or that I am in myself. I shall know vanity from truth by the light of that blessed candle which I shall hold in my hand at the hour of my death. What will it profit me then to have been esteemed and honored by the whole world, if my conscience convicts me of sin before God? Ah, what folly it would be for a nobleman, possessing talents which would endear him to his king and make him a favorite at court, if he were to seek rather to be adulated by his servants and menials, and to find pleasure in such miserable adulation. But it is a far greater folly for a Christian, who might gain the praise and honor of God and of all the Angels and Saints in Heaven, to seek rather to be praised and honored by men and to glory in it. By humility I can please God, the Angels and the Saints; therefore, is it not a despicable pride that makes me desire the esteem, praise and approbation of men, when we are told that "He is approved whom God commendeth?" (*2 Cor.* 10:18).

The thought of death is profitable in order to acquire humility; and humility helps us greatly to obtain a holy death. St. Catherine of Siena, shortly before her death, was tempted to thoughts of pride and vainglory on account of her own holiness; but to this temptation she answered: "I render thanks to God that in all my life I have never felt any vainglory." Oh, how beautiful to be able to exclaim on one's deathbed: I have never known vainglory!

88. Even admitting the value of the world's esteem and fame—for the sole reason that we love and desire it in our hearts, we can infer from this how great is the virtue of humility—since offering all that we hold so precious to God, together with our self-esteem, we offer Him something that we value very highly.

The vow of chastity is considered heroic because we thus sacrifice to God the pleasures of the senses. Martyrdom is considered heroic because the martyr thus offers up his life as a holocaust to God. And it is also considered heroic to give all one's goods to the poor. But our self-esteem is certainly what we hold more precious than either money, gratification of the senses or even life itself, because we often risk all these things for the sake of our reputation. Thus, by offering to God our self-esteem, with humility, we offer that which we deem most precious.

This is truly offering "sacrifice to God . . . and a good savour." (*Ecclus.* 45:20). Those who live in the world can often gain more merit by their humility of heart than those who are vowed to poverty and chastity in the sacred cloister, for it is by the practice of this humility that we form within ourselves the "new creature," without which St. Paul says that "Neither circumcision availeth anything, nor uncircumcision," (*Gal.* 6:15), which is as much as to say that, whether you are priest or layman, your state can avail nothing without humility.

Humility without virginity may be pleasing to God, but never virginity without humility. Were not the five foolish virgins displeasing to

Him? *Vanitate superbiæ*—"Begone, Pride!" says St. Augustine. And if the Blessed Virgin herself pleased God by her virginity, she also deserved to be chosen for His Mother because of her humility, as St. Bernard says: "By her virginity she pleased God; by her humility she conceived Him."[55]

89. It is very easy for a proud person to fall into grave and terrible sins and, after having fallen, to find great difficulty in accusing himself of them in the Sacrament of Penance. For loving his self-esteem and reputation too well and fearing to lose them in the eyes of his confessor, he would rather commit a [mortal sin of] sacrilege than disclose his weakness. He goes in search of a confessor to whom he is unknown, in order to avoid shame; but since he felt no shame in sinning, why should he feel so much shame in confessing his sin, if it be not from motives of pride?

My Soul, say to thyself: "The reason why I do not feel true sorrow for my sins is due to my lack of humility, for it is impossible for the heart to feel either attrition[56] or contrition if it is not humbled.

---

55. *"Virginitate placuit, humilitate concepit."* (Hom. 1 sup. *"Missus est"*).
56. "Attrition," as used here, means "imperfect contrition," i.e., contrition or sorrow for sins because one fears the punishment of God for them—as opposed to "contrition," or "perfect contrition," i.e., sorrow for sins because they offend God, who is infinitely good. Attrition, or imperfect contrition, is sufficient sorrow for sins in order for sins, even mortal sins, to be forgiven when it is accompanied by the Sacrament of Confession. Perfect contrition will

I lack humility, and it is for this reason that I have not the courage to confess my sins straightforwardly and without excuse." Ask God for humility, and in the measure as thy heart grows more humble, it will feel deeper sorrow for having offended Him. And from this heartfelt humility, the words will flow without difficulty to thy lips, because "He that pricketh the heart, bringeth forth resentment." (*Ecclus.* 22:24).

It is pride that compels us to withhold our sins in the confessional and seek to palliate their wickedness with many excuses. O accursed Pride, cause of innumerable sacrileges! But O blessed Humility! King David was humble in his repentance because he did not excuse his sins, but publicly accused himself of them; nor did he lay the blame of his own sins on others, but attributed them only to his own wickedness: "I am he that have sinned." (*2 Kgs.* 24:17). And the Magdalen also, in her repentance, did not seek for Jesus Christ in some hidden spot, but sought Him out in the house of the Pharisee and desired to appear as a sinner before all the guests. St. Augustine, being truly humble in his repentance, gave the confession of his sins to the whole world for his own greater confusion [humiliation] and shame.

---

earn forgiveness of our sins, including mortal sin, even if it is achieved independently of the Sacrament of Confession. But if one has committed mortal sin, he must always go to Sacramental Confession *before* he can once again receive Holy Communion worthily, even if he has perfect contrition.

90. It is difficult for us to realize our own nothingness, and it is difficult also to refer all things to God without reserving anything for ourselves, because is not our industry, our diligence and the co-operation of our will really ours? Let us admit this, but if we take away the light, the help and the grace received from God, what remains to us of all these things? Our natural actions only become meritorious when they are supernaturalized by Christ Jesus. It is Jesus Christ who raises and ennobles all our actions, which in themselves would be entirely inadequate to procure for us the glory of eternal life.

How the will is moved by grace to co-operate with grace is a mystery which we do not fully comprehend; but it is certain that, if we go to Heaven, we shall then render thanks for our salvation to the mercy of God alone: "The mercies of the Lord I will sing for ever." (*Ps.* 88:2). We may therefore say with holy King David, and be fully persuaded of its truth, that human nature is weaker and more impotent than we can imagine, because, in the nature which we have received of God, we have only, through the fall of Adam, ignorance of mind, weakness of reason, corruption of will, disorder of the passions, sickness and misery of the body. We have nothing therefore in which to glory, but in all things we can find fit cause for humiliation. "Humble thyself in all things," (*Ecclus.* 3:20), says the Holy Ghost, and He does not tell us to humble ourselves in some things only, but in *all* things—*in omnibus.*

91. Holy humility is inimical to certain subtle speculations; for instance, you say that you cannot understand how it is that you are yourself mere nothingness, in doing and being, because you cannot help knowing that in reality you are something and can do many things; that you cannot understand why you are the greatest of all sinners, because you know so many others who are greater sinners than yourself; nor how it is that you merit all the vituperations of men, when you know that you have done no actions worthy of blame, but on the contrary, many worthy of praise. You should reprove yourself for being still so far from true humility in thinking that you could grasp the meaning of these things. The truly humble believes that he is of himself mere nothingness, a greater sinner than others, inferior to all, worthy of being reviled by all as being, more than all others, ungrateful to God. He knows that this feeling of his conscience is absolutely true and does not care to investigate how this comes to be true; his knowledge is practical, and even if he does not understand himself and cannot explain to others with subtle reasoning what he feels in his heart, he minds as little being unable to explain this as he minds his inability to explain how the eye sees, the tongue speaks, the ear hears. And from this we may infer that it is not necessary to have great talents in order to be humble, and therefore before the tribunal of God, it will not be a valid excuse for us to say: "I have not been humble because I did not know, because I did not understand, because I did not study." We can have a good will, a good heart, and yet not be clever; and there is no one who cannot grasp this truth, that from God comes all the good that he possesses and that no one has anything of his own, except his own malice. "Destruction is thy own, O Israel: thy help is only in me," (*Osee* 13:9), said God by the mouth of His prophet.

92. Humility is a potent means of subduing temptation, and in the same way, temptations serve to maintain humility, because it is when we are tempted, that we are practically conscious of our own weakness and the need we have of divine grace.

It is for this reason that God permits us to fall into temptation, reducing us sometimes to the very brink of succumbing to it, so that we may learn the weakness of our virtue and how much we need the help of God.

And even in this we can see the infinite wisdom of God, who has so disposed things that the demons themselves, spirits of pride, should contribute to render us humble, if we only knew how to make good use of our temptations. Nevertheless, we must remember that, in all our temptations, the first thing is to exercise that humility which is derived from a practical knowledge of ourselves and of how prone we are to evil, if God does not stretch out His hand to restrain us through His grace. Do not let us wait to learn our weakness till we have fallen, but let us rather know it beforehand, and the knowledge of it will be an efficacious means to keep us from falling. "Before sickness take a medicine. . . . Humble thyself . . ." (*Ecclus.* 18:20-21), says Holy Writ.

The humble will never want for grace in the time of temptation, and with the help of this grace they will even derive profit from these very temptations, for the merciful providence of God has so disposed it that with the special aid of His grace He will "let no temptation take hold on you." (*1 Cor.* 10:13).

93. Let us strive with all our might to acquire this holy humility; and if by the help of God, we succeed in possessing it only in such measure as our state of life demands, we shall then either imperceptibly attain to all other virtues, or this humility alone will suffice to compensate for all our deficiencies. Many people desire to possess either chastity or charity, gentleness or patience, or some other virtue of which they are more in need, and are most anxious to know how they are to acquire it. They consult various spiritual directors to learn what means to take, but very few exercise due prudence in the choice of these means.

Do you wish to know the most efficacious means of acquiring these virtues? Then begin by endeavoring to acquire humility. Impregnate yourself with humility, and you will soon find that all other virtues will follow without any effort on your part, and you will exclaim with great joy: "Now all good things came to me together with her." (*Wis.* 7:11). And even when, through the frailty of your own nature, you are deficient in some particular virtue, humble yourself, and that humility will fully compensate for your other deficiencies.

There are some who are troubled because their prayers are full of distractions. This proceeds from pride, which is presumptuous enough to be astonished at the weakness and impotency of the mind. When you perceive that your thoughts are wandering, make an act of humility, and exclaim: "O my God, what an abject creature I am in not being able to fix my thoughts on Thee, even for a few moments." Renew this act of humility as often as these distractions occur, and if it is written of charity that it "covereth a multitude of sins," (*1 Peter* 4:8), it is also true of humility and contributes greatly to our perfection. "The very knowledge of our imperfection," says St. Augustine, "tends to the praise of humility." [57]

94. We have more opportunities of practicing humility than any other virtue. How many occasions we have of humbling ourselves secretly—in all places, at all times, at every turn—toward God, toward our fellow-men, and even toward ourselves! With regard to God, how much we have to be ashamed of in our ignorance and ingratitude

---

57. *"Ipsa imperfectionis cognitio est in humilitate confessio."*— "Literally, the very knowledge of imperfection is a confession in humility." (Lib. 3 *ad Bonif.,* c. vii).

toward Him, receiving as we do, continual benefits of His infinite goodness. Knowing as we do His supreme and infinite Majesty, deserving of all fear; His infinite goodness, worthy of all love; how much we ought to humble ourselves in the thought of how little fear and love we have for Him! With regard to our neighbor, if he be wicked, we may humble ourselves by reflecting that we are capable of becoming suddenly worse than he, and in fact we may consider ourselves worse already, if pride predominates within us. If he be good, we must humble ourselves in the thought that he corresponds better than we do to the grace of God and is better than we are by reason of his humility of heart. With regard to ourselves, we need never lack opportunities of humility when we remember our past sins, or consider the faults we commit at present in our daily life, or even when we reflect upon our good works, which are all tainted with imperfection, or when we think of the future, so filled with tremendous uncertainty. "I know how to be brought low everywhere and in all things," (*Phil.* 4:12), says St. Paul. It is necessary for us to form the good habit of frequently renewing these interior acts of humility. Humility is merely a virtuous habit, but how can we acquire this habit without making repeated acts of humility? Like the habit of humility, the habit of pride is acquired through frequent repetition of its acts, and in proportion as the habit of humility is strengthened, the contrary habit of pride becomes weakened and diminished.

95. Lucifer sinned once only, and through pride of thought. Ought we not therefore to consider ourselves worse than Lucifer, since our pride has become habitual through the frequent repetition of its acts? We do not consider ourselves proud, because it does not seem to us that we are rash enough in our minds either to believe that we resemble God or to rebel against God; but this is the greatest mistake we can make, because we are full of pride and will not recognize that we are proud. Even if we have not sufficient pride to rebel, to think or to speak against God, we must be fully aware that the pride which prompts our actions is far worse than the pride of thought, and is that pride which is so condemned by St. Paul: "They profess that they know God, but in their works they deny him." (*Titus* 1:16).

How great is our self-love! Do we ever mortify our passions for the love of God, as He Himself has commanded? How often do we prefer to follow our own will instead of the Will of God, and as His Will is contrary to our own, we place ourselves in opposition to Him and desire to gain our own will instead of fulfilling His, valuing the satisfaction of our desires more than the obedience we owe to God! Is not this a worse pride than Lucifer's? For Lucifer only wanted to make himself equal to God; whereas, we wish to raise our will above God's. Thou must humble thyself, O my Soul, even below Lucifer, and confess that thou art more proud than he!

96. We may compare ourselves to those who, suffering from foulness of breath consequent upon some disease, are rendered objectionable to those who approach them, although they are unaware of it themselves. In the same way, when we are corrupted by interior pride, we breathe the external signs of it in our words, looks and gestures, and in a thousand other ways, as occasion may arise, and yet though our pride is apparent to all who approach us, we ourselves ignore it.

I am considered proud by those who know me, and they are not mistaken, for I show it by my vanity, arrogance, petulance and haughtiness. I alone do not know myself as I am, and if I question myself: "Am I proud?" "Oh no!" I answer, offering to myself incense, which is more nauseous than all.

97. It is necessary to discern in the Gospel those things which are of counsel [advised] and those which are of precept [commanded]. To renounce all that one has and to suffer poverty for the love of God is only of counsel, but to renounce oneself and to be poor of heart is of precept. And in the same way, certain exterior humiliations may be only of counsel, but humility of heart is always of precept. And it is not only possible to fulfill every precept of God, but also, by the help of His grace, it becomes easy and sweet to us to practice them. Even laymen have many great opportunities of becoming holy, simply by the exercise of humility. To make a worldly-minded man a saint, it is sufficient to make him a Christian.

When such thoughts as the following arise in the secret recesses of the heart: "I have made this fortune by my knowledge, by my industry; I have acquired this merit, this reputation by my own worth, my virtue, my ingenuity," then it is enough to lift up one's heart to God and say with the Wise Man: "And how could anything endure, if thou wouldst not?" (*Wisdom* 11:26). O my God, how could I have done the smallest thing, if Thou hadst not willed it?

This is true humility, and in this lies true knowledge and holiness. The soul is holy in measure as it is humble, because in the same measure that it has holiness, it has grace; and in the same measure that it has grace, it has humility, because grace is only given to the humble.

From the depths of my heart, O my God, I ask it of Thee, and with the Psalmist I exclaim: "Renew a right spirit within my bowels." (*Ps.* 50:12).

98. But the greatest motive we have to oblige us to be humble is the example of Our Lord Jesus Christ, who came down from Heaven to teach us the humility of which we stood in such need to cure our pride, the cause of all our ills and the greatest impediment to our eternal salvation. "Therefore," says St. Thomas, "Christ recommended humility to us above everything else, because by this, more especially, all hindrance to the salvation of men is removed."[58]

---

58. "*Ideo Christus præcipere nobis humilitatem commendavit, quia per hanc maxime removetur impedimentum humanæ salutis.*" (*S.T.*, IIa IIæ, Q. 171, art. 5, ad 3).

And in truth He has taught us most excellently, not only by word, but by deed. Let us meditate upon the life of Our Lord on earth—from the Cave of Bethlehem to the Cross of Calvary. Everything breathes of humility! More than once did he declare in the Gospel that He came, not to fulfill His own will, but that of His heavenly Father; not to seek His own glory, but that of His heavenly Father. And as He preached, so He lived. He might have glorified the Divine Majesty in divers other ways, but in His infinite wisdom, He chose the way of humility as the most suitable one for rendering unto God, by His own humility, that honor of which the pride of man has deprived Him.

What humility, to be born in a stable—He who was the King of Glory! What humility in Him, who was innocence itself, to appear as a sinner at the Circumcision! What humility, in the Flight into Egypt, to escape the persecution of Herod, as if He had been incapable of saving Himself otherwise than by flight! What humility, in His subjection to Mary and Joseph, He who was King of the whole universe! What humility, in living for thirty years a hidden life of poverty, He who could have been surrounded by all the splendor of the world! With what humility He bore all the insults and calumnies He received in return for the truths He preached and the miracles He worked, never complaining nor lamenting those ills that were done to Him, nor the injustice that was shown to Him! Oh, if one could have looked into His Heart, one would have seen that His humility was not obligatory, but voluntary, "because it was His own will." (*Is.* 53:7).

He desired to humble Himself thus in order that we might make Him our pattern, and He says to each one of us: "For I have given you an example, that as I have done to you, so you do also," (*John* 13:15), which means that He gave us this example so that we might learn to humble ourselves even as He humbled Himself from His heart. Ah, will not these examples of a God who became man and humbled Himself suffice to rouse in us the wish to become humble also? "Let man be ashamed to be proud," says St. Augustine, "for whose sake a God became humble."[59]

99. And what lessons in humility may we not learn from the sacred Passion of Our Lord? St. Peter tells us that Jesus Christ suffered for us, leaving us His example, so that we might imitate Him: "Christ also suffered for us, leaving you an example that you should follow His steps." (*1 Peter* 2:21). He does not pretend that we ought to imitate Him by being scourged, crowned with thorns, or nailed to the Cross. No, but in all His life, and especially during His Passion, He repeats that important exhortation that we should learn of Him to be humble: "Learn of Me, because I am meek and humble of heart." (*Matt.* 11:29).

---

59. *"Tam tandem erubescat homo esse superbus propter quem factus est humilis Deus"* (*Enarr. in Ps.* 18).

My Soul, let us gaze upon the Crucified, "Who endured the cross, despising the shame," (*Heb.* 12:2), and by thus confronting His humility with our pride, we shall be filled with shame and confusion. And learn yet another lesson. Does it seem well to thee to adore the humility of Jesus crucified and not to wish to imitate Him? To profess to follow Jesus Christ in His religion, which is founded on humility, and yet to feel aversion and even hatred toward this very humility?

But when we so often hear it said and preached that whoever wishes to be saved must imitate the Saviour, in what do we imagine that this imitation should consist, which is commanded of us and which is necessary for our salvation, if not in humility? It is all very well to say that we must imitate Jesus, but in what must we imitate Him, if not in this humility, which is the summing-up of all the doctrine and examples of His life?

For that Humble One on the Cross will be our Judge; and His humility will be the standard by which it will be seen whether we shall be predestined for having imitated it, or eternally condemned for having rejected it. It is necessary for us to be firmly convinced of this truth. God does not propose that we should all imitate His Incarnate Son in all the mysteries of His life. The solitude and austerity which He endured in the desert are reserved only for the imitation of anchorites [hermits]. In His teaching, He is to be imitated only by the Apostles and preachers of His Gospel. In the working of miracles, only those can imitate Him who have been chosen by Him to be co-adjutors in the establishment of the Faith. In the sufferings and agony of Calvary, none may imitate Him but those to whom He has given the privilege of martyrdom.

But that humility of heart practiced by Jesus Christ in every hour of His life on earth is given to all of us as an example which we are compelled to follow, and to this imitation God has united our eternal salvation: "Unless you be converted and become as little children . . ." (*Matt.* 18:3).

We may believe that Jesus Christ was comparing Himself with a little child whom He had before Him when He said: "Unless you be converted and become as little children, you shall not enter into the kingdom of Heaven." (*Matt.* 18:3).

100. After Jesus Christ, who is King of the humble, what a beautiful example of humility we have in the Blessed Virgin Mary, who is their Queen! No creature ever surpassed her in merit or exceeded her in humility. By her humility she deserved to be the Mother of God, and by humility only, she maintained the dignity and honor of the sublime Maternity.

Let us picture Mary in her room at Nazareth when it was announced to her by the Archangel Gabriel that the time had come for the Eternal Word to take flesh in her womb through the operation of the Holy Ghost. She showed no sign of pride at being blessed among women and chosen for such a high honor; but on the contrary, she was distressed and "was troubled at his saying," (*Luke* 1:29), without being able to understand why she was chosen for so great an honor.

And what does she exclaim? "I, the Mother of God? I, a vile creature, to become the Mother of God? I am but His servant, and it would be too much honor for me even to be His handmaid!" [Rather, she replied], "Behold the handmaid of the Lord." (*Luke* 1:38). Thus Mary humbled herself as much as lay in her power; and she continued in this deep humility all through her life, behaving in all things as the servant of the Lord, without ever attributing to herself the slightest glory for being His Mother. What a beautiful example for us! Therefore, if we have devotion to Our Lady, we ought to try to imitate her in her humility; and in all the prayers, communions and mortifications that we offer in her honor, let us always ask her to obtain for us through her intercession the grace of holy humility. There is no grace that our Blessed Lady asks so willingly of Jesus for her devotees and which Jesus concedes so willingly to Mary as the grace of humility, since both Jesus and Mary hold this virtue in singular affection.

Let us recommend ourselves to her protection and place all our confidence in her, entreating her, for the love she herself bears to humility, to grant that we may also become truly humble of heart; and let us not doubt but that our earnest prayers will be heard and our desires granted.

O my Soul, it is through humility that we shall reach Paradise. And what shall we do in Paradise? There the practice of all other virtues ceases, and only charity and humility remain. We shall see God, and in seeing Him, we shall know that He is the infinite Good; and this perfect knowledge will bring with it more perfect love. And the more we love God, the better we shall know Him, and the better we know Him, the more humble we shall be, practicing humility through all eternity, like the ancients seen in the *Apocalypse* by the Apostle St. John: "Who fell on their faces and adored God, saying, We give Thee thanks, O Lord God almighty, who art, and who wast, and who art to come." (*Apoc.* 11:17). Let us begin to practice on earth those virtues which we hope to practice forever and ever through all ages in Heaven. "Our Lord Jesus Christ humbled Himself, becoming obedient unto death, even to the death of the cross. For which cause God also hath exalted Him, and hath given Him a name which is above all names." (*Phil.* 2:8-9). "Deliver me, O Lord, from the evil man; rescue me from the unjust man." (*Ps.* 139:2). Who is this wicked and unjust man from whom I pray to be delivered? He is my inner self, who is all vice, corruption and pride, and it is the same as if I were to say: "Deliver me, O Lord, from myself; that is, give me grace to amend and reform myself in order that I may no longer be that earthly, worldly and proud creature which I have been hitherto, dominated by passion, but that I may be renewed and may conform to the spirit of my humble Lord and Master, Jesus Christ." "Deliver me, O Lord, from the evil man; rescue me from the unjust man." (*Ps.* 139:2).

Prayer

O God, Who resistest the proud and givest Thy grace to the humble, grant us the grace of true humility, of which Thine only begotten Son showed forth in Himself an example to the faithful, that we may never, puffed up by pride, incur Thine anger, but that, submissive to Thy Will, we may receive the gifts of Thy grace.

⚮2⚮

Practical Examen on the Virtue of Humility

NOW that you are conversant with the idea of humility in its necessity, its excellence and its motives, I am persuaded that a fervent desire to practice it has been excited in your heart. But because, on the one hand, you cannot do this without the special help of God, and on the other, God will work nothing in you without you—that is, without the co-operation of your own will—it therefore follows that, when you have invoked the divine help, not doubting that you will receive it, you must apply yourself to adopt those means which are most likely to help you to attain that virtue.

And because all the masters of the spiritual life agree in this, that it is most efficacious to make a particular examen every day on the virtue which we wish to acquire, I will expound for your enlightenment a practical examen on Christian humility; and in order that you make a good use of it, I offer you three words of advice.

The *first* is that in making your examen—once a day, at least—in order to mark those faults which you may have committed against humility, you must not examine yourself each time upon every fault that you may have noted down, but begin by choosing not more than one or two of the most flagrant ones which you are in the habit of committing. And thus, after having accustomed yourself to amend these, you will pass on, little by little, to the others, until pride will gradually be eradicated and humility will spring up in your heart.

This is also the manner in which we ought to meditate. Certain general resolutions, such as to subdue pride and to practice humility, are never of any use; but on the contrary, they frequently generate confusion and create conflict in the mind. Therefore, it is necessary to go into particulars on those things in which during the day we have been most sensible of our imperfections. And even then, we must not form a general intention not to fall into them again all our life through, but it is enough that we should make a firm resolution not to fall into them again during that one day. It was thus that holy King David made resolutions and renewed them, not trying to keep them from year to year, nor from month to month, but from day to day: I will "pay my vows from day to day." (*Ps.* 60:9). And in order to keep them, one cannot sufficiently urge the necessity of imposing upon oneself some penance and of accomplishing it faithfully. For example, as many times as I have failed to keep my resolutions today, so many times will I kiss the wound in the side of Christ and recite devoutly as many Hail Marys, etc.

The *second* is to take these faults which form the subject of our examen and to accuse ourselves of them in our Confessions, in order to make us still more ashamed before God of our pride, and also because the Sacrament of Penance confers a singular grace of its own in helping us to amend those faults of which we therein accuse ourselves, as St. Thomas teaches.[1] And although none of these defects can absolutely be called sins, and are simply imperfections, it does not follow that we must not pay any heed to them, because they either serve to keep us in vice or are an impediment to virtue.

When it is a question of humility, which is the most necessary virtue for our eternal salvation, it is always better and safer to have too much of it than to have too little. And it is certain that he who is content to have only that amount which is absolutely essential to him will never really acquire that virtue. "Unless you become as little children, you cannot enter into the kingdom of heaven," said the Saviour of the world, and we have no other way of becoming as little children than to eliminate our self-love by the vigorous exercise of humility.

The *third* is that you should often read this practical examen, in order to reflect seriously upon yourself and to see how you stand in regard to humility, so that you may not be among those who think they are humble and are not really so.

---

1. *S.T.,* IIIa, Q. 84, art. 8, ad 1.

St. Thomas says that it is for humility to examine the faults committed against any virtue whatsoever. How much more, therefore, should it examine those faults which are committed against this very humility!

You will find many little points in this examen, but if you find yourself defective in many of them, you must not regard them from the point of view of their size, but of their number, and the more you find that they are habitual with you, the more they should fill you with fear and apprehension. And in proportion as you find that you are not humble in this point or that, you will be able to infer that you are proud; and if this examen on humility only teaches you to know your own pride, it will not be a small gain, because we begin to be humble when we open our eyes and recognize that we are proud.

Many things considered in themselves are only of counsel [advised]; but in respect to such and such circumstances, they can nevertheless be of obligation and are necessary also so that we may not transgress the precept [commandment], according to the teaching of St. Thomas.[2] In conclusion, you must not make this examen with scruples or much anxiety, as if every imperfection were a sin and as if you had the presumption to will to be humble all at once, nor must you reject with contempt all that does not seem to you positively of precept [commandment].

---

2. IIa IIæ, Q. 72, art. 3; et Q. 186, art. 2.

You must be solicitous in your wish and desire to acquire humility, and you should have diligence and care not to omit those means which would lead you to gain it. And then, recommending yourself to God, continue to make this examen according to the inspiration of God and the dictates of your own conscience. As humility may be considered under three different aspects—in relation to God, our neighbor and ourselves—and practiced in two ways, that is to say, interiorly and exteriorly, it therefore follows that we can sin in these several ways, as we sin against the laws of any other virtue, either by our thoughts, words, deeds or omissions. Let us therefore proceed now to the examen of our faults.

∽3∼

Examen on Humility Toward God

THE first act of humility, says St. Thomas,[1] consists in rendering ourselves entirely subject to God, with the greatest reverence for His infinite Majesty, before which we are as nothing: "All nations are before him as if they had no being at all." (*Is.* 40:17). But do you ever consider your nothingness before God; and that all the being you have, you have from God; and that through intrinsic necessity you depend so entirely upon God that without Him you cannot do anything good—"for without me you can do nothing" (*John* 15:5)—that without God you neither think nor say nor do anything that is good?

This is of faith: "No man can say the Lord Jesus, but by the Holy Ghost." (*1 Cor.* 12:3). "Not that we are sufficient to think anything of ourselves, as of ourselves: but our sufficiency is from God." (*2 Cor.* 3:5). "For it is God who worketh in you, both to will and to accomplish, according to his good will." (*Phil.* 2:13). It is not enough only to say I know all these things, but it is necessary to *realize* them, in order to become really humble.

---

1. *S.T.,* IIa IIæ, Q. 161, art. 2, ad 3; et Q. 162, art. 5.

The Angelic Doctor teaches that the reason why humility tends principally to render the soul subject to God is that this virtue is nearest to the theological virtues, and as it does not suffice only to know what things we must believe or hope, but it is also necessary for us to make *acts* of faith and hope, so in the same way we must make like acts of humility.

Christ Himself taught humility of heart, and the heart must not remain idle, nor fail to produce the necessary acts. And what acts of humility do you make before God? How often do you make them? When have you made them? How long is it since you made them?

It would be absurd to hope for the reward which is promised to the humble without being humble, or at least without the desire to be humble, and without making acts of humility; humility of heart without the heart's humbling itself—what folly! And are you foolish enough to believe that this can be done?

Sometimes you give utterance to certain words which seem to tend to your own humiliation; you say you are a contemptible wretch and good for nothing, but do you say such things sincerely from your heart? If you are afraid of lying to yourself by confirming them in your own mind, listen to what St. Thomas[2] tells us for our instruction, that everyone can truthfully say and believe of himself that he is a contemptible wretch, referring all his

---

2. *Loc. cit.* art. 6, ad 1.

ability and talent to God.

103. But how are we to make these practical acts of humility before God? I will give you some examples. You can imagine yourself in the presence of God, now as a convicted felon who humbles himself and implores mercy for the forgiveness of his sins: "Have mercy upon me, O God, according to Thy great mercy." (*Ps.* 50:1). Now as a miserable, needy beggar who humbles himself and asks alms to help him in his necessity: "Give us this day our daily bread." Now as the sick man near the Pool of Bethsaida, who humbled himself before the Saviour, to be healed of his incurable disease: "Sir, I have no man . . . to put me into the pond." (*John* 5:7). Now as that blind man who humbled himself, that his darkness might be illuminated: "Lord, that I may see." Now as the Canaanite woman who humbled herself and exclaimed: "Have mercy on me, O Lord, . . . help me," (*Matt.* 15:22-25), and who was not ashamed to liken herself to the dogs who are unworthy to eat their master's bread, but are content to eat the crumbs that fall from his table. Humility of heart is ingenuous, and in the same manner as our heart loves without needing to be taught to love, it humbles itself without needing to be taught humility.

104. There are certain cases in which we are obliged to make acts of virtue—such as faith, hope and charity—which some necessity, circumstance, or duty of our state of life may exact, and there are certain cases in which we must make acts of humility in our hearts.

First of all, it is necessary to humble ourselves when we approach God with prayer to obtain some grace, because God does not regard nor heed nor impart His grace except to the humble. "The Lord is high and looketh on the low." (*Ps.* 137:6). "The prayer of the humble and the meek hath always pleased Thee," (*Judith* 9:16). "God giveth grace to the humble." (*James* 4:6). When, therefore, you come to ask God for some grace of the body or of the soul, do you always remember to practice this humility?

When we pray, and especially when we say the "Our Father," we are speaking to God; and how many times when you are saying your prayers, do you speak to God with less respect than if you were speaking to one of your fellow creatures? How often when you are in church, which is the house of God, do you listen to a sermon, which is the Word of God, and assist at the functions of the service without any reverence?

Humility of heart, says St. Thomas,[3] is accompanied by exterior reverence; and to be lacking in this is to lack humility and is therefore a sin of pride, "which excludes reverence."

105. But the more essential for us is the grace that we are asking of God, the more necessary is

---

3. *S.T.,* IIa IIæ, Q. 161, art. 2.

humility. However, before going to the tribunal of Penance, do you humble yourself and ask God to give you that sorrow for your sins which is necessary for the validity of the Sacrament? As this sorrow must be supernatural, it is certain that you could never attain to it of yourself, however much you were to try to force yourself to feel it. God alone can give it to you, and it is equally certain that this is not a debt which He owes you, but a great grace which it pleases Him to confer upon you out of His goodness alone and without any merit on your part. If, however, you desire to receive this grace, you must ask for it with humility, protesting from your heart that you do not deserve it, that you are unworthy to receive it, and that you only hope for it through the merits of Jesus Christ. But do you practice this humility, which one may say is of precept [commandment] for you, because it is an essential means of obtaining contrition?

106. The same can be said of your resolutions, which are equally necessary to render the Confession valid. These resolutions must be constant and efficacious, but cannot be so without the special help of God. Do you ever think of humbling yourself and asking for that help, knowing and confessing your instability and weakness, and that you are not capable of yourself to keep the smallest resolution, either from morning till night, or even from one hour to another?

It is for this reason that you so often fall, over

and over again, into the same faults, because you are lacking in humility. The truly humble man is altogether diffident [mistrustful] about himself and, putting all his trust in God, is helped in the most admirable way by Him. "Humble thyself to God and wait for his hands." (*Ecclus.* 13:9).

How many times do you not say: "I have taken this firm resolution, and I mean to keep it; I am not afraid of breaking it," trusting iniquitously in yourself, without acknowledging the divine help in any way? Take care that you may not be counted among those reprobates "who were destroyed, trusting to their own strength." (*Ecclus.* 16:8). If you even presume only a little upon yourself, that little can be the cause of great ruin, according to the prediction of Job: "They are lifted up for a little while and shall not stand, and shall be brought down." (*Job* 24:24).

107. And how do you practice humility in your sacramental Confession? It is in your Confession that you should humble yourself like a guilty malefactor in the presence of your Judge: "Humble thy soul to the ancient." (*Ecclus.* 4:7). This advice comes from the Holy Ghost.

How often do you not try to appear innocent in the very act of accusing yourself of guilt—now by excusing your sins, now by covering or diminishing their malice, now by putting the blame on others, instead of taking it yourself? This is a real lack of humility, and of that humility which is not of counsel but of precept. You should say with

David: "I said I will confess against myself my injustice to the Lord." (*Ps.* 31:5). The shame which prevents you from confessing your sin clearly and plainly comes from pride alone.

108. There are some people who, under the pretext of making acts of humility, desire from time to time to accuse themselves in their Confession of some grave and shameful sin of their past life. If perhaps you are among these, beware lest this arise more from a desire to appear humble than to be humble in reality. Self-love is cunning and knows how to work secretly.

This fault was discovered by St. Bernard: "The more subtly vain Confession is, the more dangerously hurtful it is, as when, for instance, we are not ashamed to reveal our shameful deeds, not because we are humble, but that we may seem to be so. What is more perverse or shameful than that Confession, the guardian of humility, should take service under the banner of pride?"[4]

This kind of humility is not always desirable, even outside the confessional, because it can easily lead us to create scandal by speaking of certain sins which should not even be named. If you have this strange fault, there is no reason why you should pride yourself on it, but you should

---

4. *"Est confessio eo periculosius noxia quo subtilius vana, cum etiam ipsa turpia de nobis detegere non veremur, non quia humiles sumus sed ut esse putemur. Quid perversius indigniusve quam ut humilitatis custos, confessio, superbiæ militet?"* (*Serm. 6 in Cant.*).

rather be ashamed of it; for, as the holy abbot [St. Bernard] says: "What species of pride can this be, that you would gladly seem to be better by what you appear to be worse? That you cannot be thought holy without seeming to be wicked?"[5]

109. And also, after Confession, you must remember the sins you have committed, in order to excite your heart to feelings of shame and sorrow, humbling yourself before God. But do you remember to exercise yourself in this humility? This is a humility of precept [commandment]. "The whole life of the Christian must be one long penance."[6] Thus speaks the holy Council of Trent, where the whole Church of Christ was assembled, and its dogmas are infallible, not less in matters of morality than in those of faith.

The Council of Trent says "must be," which is a formula, not of exhortation, but of necessity; and it does not prescribe such penances as scourgings, hair shirts or fasts, but speaks generally; and we cannot interpret the sense of these words with more discretion than by saying: "If you cannot perform certain exterior penances, you must nevertheless never neglect those interior penances which consist in the contrition and humiliation of the heart, saying with David: 'Have mercy upon me, O God . . . against Thee only have I sinned. . . .

---

5. *"Quale jactantiæ genus ut velis inde videri deterior? Ut non possis putari sanctus, nisi appareas sceleratus?"*

6. *"Tota vita christiana perpetua debet esse pœnitentia"* (Sess. 1, cap. 2).

A contrite and a humbled heart, O God, thou wilt not despise.'" (*Ps.* 50:19). Do you practice this penitential humility? O my God! Your sins are so numerous, and yet you live in absolute forgetfulness of them, as if you were innocent! ["Be not without fear about sin forgiven, and add not sin upon sin. And say not: The mercy of the Lord is great; he will have mercy on the multitude of my sins."—*Ecclesiasticus* 5:5-6].

Do you remember the obligation you are under to think often: "What have I done? What great evil have I done to offend God?" Pray to God that He may give you light to know the gravity of your sins, and you will have that continual sorrow which King David had, if you can say with him: "I acknowledge my iniquities."

110. Your own faith can teach you how necessary humility is in order that you should approach Holy Communion worthily. But in your preparation for that divine Sacrament and in your thanksgiving, do you make due acts of humility? It is true that you kneel down in all exterior humility and beat your breast at the *"Domine non sum dignus,"* but have you really that true humility of heart which is becoming to such a holy function?

The centurion was sanctified when he received Jesus Christ into his own house, because he prepared himself with deep humility to receive Him and said, more from his heart than with his lips, "Lord, I am not worthy that Thou shouldst enter under my roof." (*Matt.* 8:8). This mystery, more than others, calls for humility, and when the Son of God took flesh in the womb of the Blessed Virgin Mary, it was especially by virtue of her humility, "because He hath regarded the humility of His handmaid." (*Luke* 1:48). Oh, if you were to reflect that it is God you are going to receive, but do you think of this as God Himself exhorts you to do? "Be still and see that I am God." (*Ps.* 45:11).

111. How do you humble your intellect in regard to the mysteries of the Catholic Faith? Are you curious in seeking and wishing to know the reasons for those things which the Church proposes for your belief, inclining to surrender yourself more to human reasoning than to Divine authority? In matters of faith, it is most necessary to practice humility, and the more humble our belief, the more honor it gives to God.

It is for this reason that Holy Writ, after having said that God is honored by the humble, exhorts us emphatically to humble our intellect: "He is honored by the humble. Seek not the things that are too high for thee, and search not into things which are above thy ability: but the things that God hath commanded thee, think on them always, and in many of his works be not curious." (*Ecclus.* 3:22). When it is a question of faith, the Apostle teaches us that we must not seek to know the why and wherefore, but to humble any height of our understanding in lowly reverence to Jesus Christ, "bringing into captivity every understanding unto the obedience of Christ." (*2 Cor.* 10:5).

This is most necessary.

And especially when we have temptations against faith, it is necessary that we should humble ourselves immediately, without entering into argument or dispute with the devil. But are you prudent in taking these measures at once, and do you say with King David, I will not pause to consider these speculations in "great matters nor in wonderful things above me?" (*Ps.* 130:2).

112. But if we are bound to humble our intellect in the things that touch our belief, we must not humble our will the less, in order to do those things which are commanded of us. In this the substance of true humility principally consists, but how do you observe it? Do you humble yourself promptly in obedience to the divine commandments, persuaded that you are placed in this world only to do the Will of God and not your own? When you recite the "Our Father," what thought do you give to these words, "Thy will be done?" (*Matt.* 6:10). How often do you say them only with your lips and not from your heart?

113. When you attempt to disobey any of the divine commandments, how do you behave? It is especially in the time of temptation that humility is necessary. Every time the devil tempts you to commit some grave sin, he tempts you to revolt against God and to despise and offend Him.

114. How do you resign your will to the Will of

God in the time of adversity, which is especially the time when we ought to humble ourselves, as the Holy Ghost tells us by the mouth of St. Peter: "Be thou humbled therefore under the mighty hand of God?" (*1 Peter* 5:6).

As all the troubles of this world are ordained by God, and yours are sent to you by Him especially to humble your pride and keep you in due humility, do you really receive them with such intention as to correspond with the intention of God, saying with the Prophet, "It is good for me that thou hast humbled me"? (*Ps.* 118:71).

The best means to oblige God to deliver us from our troubles is to humble ourselves, and in *Psalm* 114:3,6 King David testifies to this by his own experience: "I met with trouble and sorrow . . . I was humbled and He delivered me." Do you ever practice this means of humbling yourself in your troubles, protesting that you have merited them, and deserve them, if for no other reason than on account of your pride?

God sends adversity to you to humble you, and He humbles you, so that from this humiliation you may learn humility. But what fruit of humility have you gathered from all the adversity you have hitherto had? Can you say, as Moses said to the Hebrews: "We have rejoiced for the days in which thou hast humbled us"? (*Ps.* 89:15).

115. If you have any good quality, either physical or spiritual, and if you have done any good work, do you recognize that it all comes from God, attributing all the glory to God, as due to Him alone? "To the only God be honor and glory." (*1 Tim.* 1:17). In this, says St. Paul, we discern the spirit of God, which is the spirit of humility, from the spirit of the world, which is the spirit of pride, because whoever has the spirit of God acknowledges that all that he has is simply a gift from God. "Now we have received not the spirit of this world, but the Spirit that is of God, that we may know the things that are given us from God." (*1 Cor.* 2:12).

But of what use would this recognition be, that everything comes from God, except to refer all things to Him and to thank Him? Do you thank God for the many blessings which you are constantly receiving from Him—from your very heart, with true humility, believing yourself to be so miserable that you would fall into every sin, and even into Hell itself, if God did not come to your help? "Unless the Lord had been my helper, my soul had almost dwelt in hell." (*Ps.* 93:17).

Nothing is so contrary to true humility as to seek one's own esteem in the exercise of good works. Do you sometimes do good from motives of human respect, in order to be seen—esteemed? "Take heed," Christ says to you, "that you do not your justice before men, to be seen by them." (*Matt.* 6:1). You are merely robbing God of glory, when from the gifts He has given you, you reserve some of the glory for yourself. Examine your intentions; are they purely directed to the glorification of God?

And granted that in doing good you do not seek the esteem of men, do you sometimes do this in order not to lose the good graces and favors of others, conforming to their spirit, which is to live according to the usage of the world in the forgetfulness of God? This is also loving the glory of the world more than the glory of God and is a fault which is greatly opposed to humility, and which was condemned in those chief men among the Jews who believed in Christ, but from fear of the Pharisees and out of respect to their opinion did not dare to confess Him, "for they loved the glory of men more than the glory of God." (*John* 12:43).

117. Have you perhaps a conscience which is timorous [fearful] by reason of many scruples? If such be the case, examine yourself, and you will probably find that the true reason for your scruples lies in your self-love, that is, in your pride.

You are indocile, and you do not know how to submit to that which your directors tell you to do; and St. Thomas teaches that this is an effect of pride, "because docility is the beautiful daughter of humility and disposes the soul to obedience."[7]

How is it, when we read the lives of the Saints, we do not find that they were agitated by these scruples? The Saints were humble, and where humility is, there also is tranquility of mind. We know that many scrupulous persons have been cured of their scruples, which were considered

---

7. *S.T.,* IIa IIæ, Q. 48; et Q. 49, art. 3 ad 4.

almost incurable, by no other means than by saying to God with their whole heart: "I accuse myself of pride; I am sorry for my pride, and I ask Thy help in order to amend my great pride."

But if you find that you are scrupulous less from indocility than from cowardice, go for advice once more to St. Thomas, who teaches that this cowardice also comes from pride, because in judging one's own sufficiency, we set our own judgment in opposition to that of others.[8]

Do you wish to enjoy the peace of a quiet conscience and also of certain spiritual consolations, which are a great help in aiding you to do willingly all that is necessary to lead a devout life and to be ever more fervent in the service of God? I cannot give you better advice than this: Give yourself to humility, and God will fill your soul with ineffable consolation. "And my spirit hath rejoiced," says the Blessed Virgin in her canticle; and she adds for your instruction that this exultation was sent to her by God because of her humility: "Because he hath regarded the humility of his handmaid." (*Luke* 1:48).

118. If you have a sincere wish to save your soul, you must take those means which God has ordained for you, and the principal and most essential one is humility, as is shown in Holy Scripture: "For Thou wilt save the humble people." (*Ps.* 17:28). "And He will save the humble of

---

8. *S.T.*, IIa IIæ, Q. 133, art. 1.

spirit." (*Ps.* 33:19). "Glory shall uphold the humble of spirit." (*Prov.* 29:23). And how do you esteem this humility? How do you practice it? How fervently do you ask God for it? Do you hold it to be of precept [command], or only of counsel [advice], which you are at liberty to choose or reject at will? The entrance to Paradise is not only narrow, but low; therefore, Jesus Christ said: "Unless you become as little children, you shall not enter into the kingdom of Heaven." (*Matt.* 18:3). And into this kingdom he alone can enter who "shall humble himself." (*Matt.* 18:4).

There is always danger on the journey toward our heavenly home for those who hold their heads high, and it is safer to keep them bowed low. This is a general rule for all.

St. John Chrysostom warns us: "When Our Lord said, 'Learn of Me, because I am meek and humble of heart,' it was not merely to monks that He spoke, but to all classes of men."[9]

Humility of heart was not commanded by Jesus Christ only to religious, but also to seculars, whoever they may be and without any exception.

---

9. "*Cum dixit Dominus, Discite a me, quia mitis sum et humilis corde, non monachos tantum alloquitur, sed et omne prorsus hominum genus. Omnes omnino hoc imperio convenit, nullum excepit.*" (*Lib.* 3).

❦ 4 ❧

Examen on Humility Toward Our Neighbor

ACCORDING to the doctrine of St. Thomas[1] the first act of humility consists in subjecting ourselves to God, and the next is to subject—that is to say, to humble—ourselves toward our neighbor for the love of God. As the Holy Ghost says through St. Peter: "Be ye subject therefore to every human creature for God's sake." (*1 Peter* 2:13). And the same Holy Spirit exhorts us through St. Paul to excel each other in humility. "In humility, let each esteem others better than themselves." (*Phil.* 2:3).

120. Now, as your neighbor can be either your superior, your equal or your inferior, it is certain that you must practice humility, first of all toward your superior, which is of precept, for as St. Peter says, such is the Will of God: "For so is the will of God." (*1 Peter* 2:15).

Do you show to your superiors and betters that obedience and reverence which your state exacts? How do you receive their reprimands? Do you feel that humility of heart toward them

1. *S.T.,* IIa IIæ, Q. 161, art. 3.

153

"with a good will serving" (*Eph.* 6:7) which St. Paul enjoins?

There is a humility necessary for the imitation of Christ, "Who humbled Himself, becoming obedient unto death." (*Phil.* 2:8). There may sometimes be an excuse of impotence or inadvertence in not obeying those whom God has set over you, but to refuse to obey is always an act of inexcusable pride. As St. Bernard says: "To be unwilling to obey is the proud effort of the will."[2]

121. How do you behave toward your equals? Do you wish to be above them, to be preferred before them, not contented with your own state? Every time that you feel this desire in your heart, say to yourself that this was the sin of Lucifer, who said in his heart: "I will ascend." (*Is.* 14:14). And St. Thomas teaches that the virtue of humility consists essentially in moderating this desire to exalt ourselves above others.

Do you esteem yourself above others for any gift of nature, education or grace? That is true pride, and you must subdue this by humility, holding yourself inferior to others, as in fact you may be before God.

122. How do you behave toward your inferiors? It is toward these that you must exercise humility most of all. "The greater thou art," says the

---

2. *S.T.,* IIa IIæ, Q. 161, art. 2.

Inspired Word, "the more humble thyself in all things." (*Ecclus.* 3:20). And though they are inferior regarding their condition in life, remember always that before God they are your equals. "Knowing that the Lord both of them and you is in heaven, and there is no respect of persons with Him." (*Eph.* 6:9).

In this way you will become kind and considerate, as St. Paul advises when he says: "Consenting to the humble." (*Rom.* 12:16). Do you command them haughtily and imperiously, against the express wish of God, who does not desire you to behave toward your inferiors "as lording it?" (*1 Peter* 5:3). And when you are obliged to correct them, do you do it in the proper spirit: "In the spirit of meekness," as the Apostle teaches us, "considering thyself, lest thou also be tempted?" (*Gal.* 6:1).

There is also another kind of humility which is false, and against which we are warned by the Holy Ghost when He says: "Be not lowly in thy wisdom, lest being humbled, thou be deceived into folly." (*Ecclus.* 13:11). If you possess the talent of teaching, counseling, helping and doing good to the souls of others, and you then retire, saying as if from humility, "I am not good enough;" or if you are in a position when it is your duty to correct, punish or exercise authority, and you abandon it from motives of humility, this is not true humility, but weakness and cowardice. And as far as externals are concerned, we must observe the rule of the holy father St. Augustine: "Lest whilst humility is unduly observed, the authority of the ruler be undermined among those who ought to be submissive."[3]

Much as I should praise you for regarding yourself as inferior in merit to all those below you, "in the knowledge of your heart," as St. Gregory says so well, yet it must not be to the detriment of your office, lessening its superiority. For being in a superior position does not prevent you from being humble of heart, but this humility must not be an impediment to the exercise of your authority.

The quotation from St. Augustine is referred to by St. Thomas: "In secret look upon others as your superiors, to whom in public you are superior."[4]

123. We have to practice two kinds of humility toward all our neighbors—one is of knowledge, the other of affection. The humility of knowledge consists in recognizing and holding ourselves in our inmost soul to be inferior to all, and that is why Jesus Christ advises us in His Gospel to take the lowest place: "Sit down in the lowest place." (*Luke* 14:10). He does not tell us to sit down in a place in the middle, nor in one of the last, but in the last; that is, we ought to have such an opinion of ourselves that we must esteem ourselves inferior to all, as St. Bernard exclaims:

---

3. *"Ne apud eos quos oportet esse subjectos, dum nimium servatur humilitas regendi frangatur auctoritas"* (In Reg.).

4. *"Existimate alios in occulto superiores, quibus estis in manifesto majores"* (*S.T.*, IIa IIae, Q. 161, art. 6, ad 1).

"That thou shouldst take thy seat alone and least of all, not only not putting thyself before others, but not even daring to compare thyself with others."[5]

The reason is that you do not know but that those whom you deem inferior to yourself, and above whom you exalt yourself, may not be far more dear to God and be placed hereafter at the right hand of the Highest.

The truly humble man believes that everyone is better than himself, and that he is the worst of all. But are you really humble like this in your own opinion? You easily compare yourself with this one and that one, but to how many do you not prefer yourself with the pride of the Pharisee: "I am not as the rest of men." (*Luke* 18:11). When you prefer yourself to others, it often seems as if you speak with a certain humility and modesty, saying, "By the grace of God, I have not the vices of such a one: By the grace of God I have not committed so many grievous sins as such a one." But is it really true that you recognize that you owe all this to the grace of God and that you give Him the glory rather than to yourself? If you esteem yourself more highly than such a one, and if he in his turn esteems himself inferior to you, he is therefore humbler than you, and for that reason better. If by the grace of God you are chaste, charitable and just, you must

5. *"Ut solus, videlicet omnium novissimus, sedeas, teque nemini non dico præponas, sed nec comparare præsumas"* (Serm. 37 *in Cant.*).

endeavor by that same grace to be humble as well. And how can you be humble if you have such an abundance of self-esteem, preferring yourself to others?

When St. Paul teaches us that in holy humility we must believe all others to be better than our-selves, he also teaches us the way to accomplish this, namely, not by considering the good we have in ourselves, but that which others have or may have: "each one not considering the things that are his own, but those that are other men's." (*Phil.* 2:4). Upon this St. Thomas founds this doctrine, that all the evil that is in man and is done by man comes from man, and that all the good that is in man and is done by man comes from God; and for four reasons he says that we may unhesitatingly affirm that everyone is better than we are:

The *first reason* is to consider in our hearts what really belongs to us, namely, malice and wickedness, and to consider what our neighbor possesses that is of God, namely, his innumerable benefits. The *second* is to consider some particular good quality which that person may have and which we have not. The *third* is to recognize some fault in ourselves which that other person has not. The *fourth* is to possess a wise fear that there may be some secret pride within us which corrupts our holiest actions and that we may be mistaken in the opinion we have of ourselves, imagining our-selves to be virtuous when we are not.[6]

---

6. *S.T.,* IIa IIæ, Q. 161, art. 3 in 4; dist. 25, Q. 2, art. 3, ad 2.

124. The humility of affection consists in the recognition that we are more miserable than anyone else, and to love to be regarded as such by others. To be vile and abject in our own eyes through the knowledge that we have of ourselves is the humility of necessity, to which we are compelled by the obvious truth of it. But to have a sincere desire to be looked upon as vile and abject by others, this is true and virtuous humility of the heart. "This is of necessity, that is, of the will," says St. Bernard, and he adds: "I fear lest in some respects that he whom truth humbles, the will should extol."[7] Take heed lest, while you do not esteem yourself, you should still wish to be esteemed by others. This would be to love something that does not exist, to love a lie.

How far you are from that humility of affection! How you fear lest any of your faults should be revealed, and how many excuses and justifications you make, in order that this imputation of a fault which you have really committed may not diminish the esteem in which others hold you. In order to be more esteemed, you try to show your ability and talent, and if you have but little ability and little talent, how often you pretend you have more, in the hope of being esteemed still more!

And since, far from loving self-abasement, you have such a desire to gain the esteem of others,

---

7. *"Illud necessitatis est, hoc voluntatis. Timeo ne quem humiliat veritas extollat voluntas"* (Serm. 42 *in Cant.*).

you belong truly to those proud sons of Adam, of whom the Prophet cried: "Why do you love vanity, and seek after lying?" (*Ps.* 4:3). Confess the truth to your own conscience, that you have more pride than humility and that you love vanity better than truth.

125. It is this humility of affection, this humility of the heart taught us by Jesus Christ, which makes us as little children and enables us to enter into the kingdom of Heaven. But what shame for you if, when you examine yourself, you find you have not even the shadow of such humility! If you happen to hear that others have spoken uncharitably of you and maligned you, are you not perturbed, disquieted, grieved, displeased, distressed? How you resent it when you think someone has wronged you or not treated you with proper respect! Are you suspicious, easily offended and punctilious about all things that concern your honor and dignity? I am not speaking now of that honor which is founded on virtue, but of that despicable honor which depends on the opinion of the world. What value do you set upon this honor? Do you take offense easily, considering yourself injured by every little adverse word, every slight that you receive from others, becoming angry and irritated, nourishing aversion and rancor, demanding humble apologies and satisfaction, and showing yourself unforgiving and irreconcilable toward them: fearing to lose your dignity if you consented to make peace like a good

Christian? If such be the case, where is your humility, either of knowledge or affection, which is necessary for your salvation?

126. In order to know to what extent you are lacking in humility, examine yourself from this point of view. The humble man not only is not angry with those who offend him, but loves them and gives them back good for evil. Yes, it is indeed so, because he looks upon them as instruments of the mercy and justice of God, and he is also persuaded that his sins and ingratitude toward the divine Goodness deserve far worse punishment. And you?

The humble man, when he hears that people are speaking ill of him, is not disturbed, but quietly learns to amend his ways, even though he may not have committed the faults of which he has been accused. He does not lament as if he were persecuted; he does not say that those who speak thus of him are malignant and jealous rivals; but he believes that they know him better than he knows himself. Do you do this?

The humble man, when he is reproved, receives the correction in good part and thanks him who has had the kindness and goodness to give it. He does not judge or speak evil of anyone, because he believes that everyone is better than he is, and because he knows he is capable of doing worse things still. He lives in peace with all and respects all and, without expecting to be honored himself, he is the first to honor others, as the holy Apostles

Peter and Paul have commanded: "Having peace with all men." (*Rom.* 12:18). "With honour preventing [i.e., anticipating] one another." (*Rom.* 12:10). "Honour all men." (*1 Peter* 2:17). And you—what can you say of yourself?

Perhaps you may imagine that these things are points of perfection; but they are points of humility, which as far as you are concerned, may be of precept. When it is a question of humility, I should not like you to imagine that you need only to reach that point which is absolutely necessary for you, without going a single hair's breadth beyond it.

When you say to yourself, "I am not obliged to do this or that act of humility," it may be that you are making a great mistake. However much your exterior humility must be directed by prudence, you certainly cannot dispense with the interior humility of the heart.

127. If the humble man becomes aware that he has offended or injured his neighbor, he immediately humbles himself, apologizes and asks to be forgiven, manifesting sorrow for the offense he has given. The humble man always fears to be dictatorial when carried away by his zeal, and therefore he proceeds with much circumspection, exercising his zeal more on himself than on others. He gives his opinion modestly, and submits it to that of others without obstinacy. But you?

The humble man respects and reverences those above him, and he is kind and courteous to the poorest of the poor; and in this he only follows the teaching of the Preacher: "Make thyself affable to the congregation of the poor, and humble thy soul to the ancient." (*Ecclus.* 4:7). Is this the way in which you generally behave?

The humble man does not seek to appear humble by affectation of manner; on the contrary, if he knows that others believe him to be humble, he feels a painful confusion. His nature is to be sincere, simple and straightforward. He is of lowly bearing, and lowly too has he kept his human caprices and his pride. He is not hard and haughty, but gentle, reverent and obedient. And you?

Ah, try to realize how backward you are in the school of Jesus Christ! He came to teach you one single lesson, that of humility: "Learn of Me, because I am meek and humble of heart." (*Matt.* 11:29). And hitherto how have you profited by this lesson? You will reply that many of these practices seem very difficult to you, but say to yourself: "The impure find it difficult to live in chastity; the avaricious find it difficult to give alms; and in the same way, the proud man finds it difficult to practice humility." It is not that humility be difficult of itself, but it is your pride that makes it difficult, and we may say with Eusebius: "You make the yoke of the Lord heavy for yourselves."[8]

---

8. *"Jugum Domini ipsi vobis facitis grave."* (Hom. de Machab.).

∽5∽

Examen on Humility Toward Oneself

RICHARD of St. Victor defines humility as the interior contempt of oneself.[1] Examine a little whether you have this feeling toward yourself. When you have dreams of dignity and honor and you imagine yourself in the midst of grandeur and chimerical honors, how do you behave in these proud and vain imaginings? Do you rejoice and delight in them, desiring to dwell in them more and more? If we love humility, we must treat these dreams of worldly ambition and pride with disdain and hatred, just as those who love chastity treat impure thoughts. We ought to pray thus with King David: "Let not the foot of pride come unto me," (*Ps.* 35:12), because pride first enters into the soul through the thoughts of the mind, and he who accustoms himself to delight in these thoughts has already formed in his heart the bad habit of pride.

129. Do you forget your own nothingness? Have you any self-esteem? If such be the case, you are

---

1. *"Humilis est qui seipsum apud semetipsum veraciter contemnit."* (*Lib.* 2, cap. 23, *De Epul. inter Hom.*).

a seducer, a deceiver of your own self, because, as St. Paul says, "For if any man think himself to be some thing, whereas he is nothing, he deceiveth himself." (*Gal.* 6:3). Do you delight and glory in your knowledge, your power, your riches, or in some other gift, natural or moral? Remember the word God spoke by the Prophet Jeremias: "Let not the wise man glory in his wisdom, and let not the strong man glory in his strength, and let not the rich man glory in his riches." (*Jer.* 9:23). And again, that spoken of by St. Paul: "We ought not to please ourselves." (*Rom.* 15:1).

This delight and glory insinuates itself insensibly, but he who is humble notices it quickly and repels it as being nothing but vanity and only puffing up and filling the heart with pride.

In the same way with the spiritual life, do you think yourself virtuous because you sometimes do a little good? You would do well then not to regard yourself as good, but to imagine yourself in Jerusalem, repudiated by God, because, as the prophet said, thou art "trusting in thy beauty." (*Ezech.* 16:15). And St. Gregory says of such as you: "The soul hath confidence in its beauty when it takes some good action upon itself."[2]

The proud man dwells more willingly on the little good he does, on the little devotion he feels, than on the thought of the evil he has committed and which he does daily. He puts behind him the

---

2. *"Fiduciam pulchritudine sua anima habet quæ in scipsa de justa actione præsumit."* (*Epist.* 126).

multitude of his sins, so that he need not be ashamed and humble himself; and he reflects often upon certain of his minute exercises of Christian piety, so as to indulge his self-complacency. As St. Gregory says: "It is easier for them to see within themselves that which is pleasing to them than that which is displeasing."[3] Perhaps you also have this tendency.

130. Humility teaches us also to hold ourselves unworthy of any good that we may possess, even to the very air that we breathe, and to hold ourselves worthy of all the evils and vituperations of the world. Such are the thoughts of the humble man. He always keeps before his eyes the sins he has committed and his malicious tendency to commit them again. Therefore, he esteems himself worse than the Turks, who have not the light of grace, while he has also that of faith; worse than all sinners, who do not realize the gravity of sin and who have not received so much help of grace as he has; worse than the Jews, "For if they had known it, they would never have crucified the Lord of glory," (*1 Cor.* 2:8); worse even than the demons, who sinned only once, in thought, whereas he has sinned so often, even in action. But do you ever stop to consider these things seriously?

---

3. *"Plus eis intueri libet quod sibi in se placet quam quod sibi in se displicet."* (Lib. 22, Mor. c. 1).

131. Do you place yourself in dangerous occasions, saying: "I will not fall into sin," thus presuming too much on your own strength? St. Gregory says that there is nothing further from humility than such a presumption. "Nothing in man is further removed from humility than reliance upon his own virtue."[4] Are you disturbed and agitated at the thought of the faults you commit and of your slow progress in acquiring virtue? This is pride and comes from your presumption in thinking you can do great things of your own strength. But it is necessary to humble ourselves and yet not be discouraged, but to learn of St. Augustine, who says of himself: "The more I lack, the more humble I shall be."[5] I shall be more humble if I reflect upon those virtues which I ought to have and have not.

Are you prudent, not trusting in your own ingenuity nor in your own opinions, [but] without caring to ask advice, especially in matters of great importance? This is a great sin against humility, and the Holy Ghost thus admonishes you: "Lean not upon thy own prudence . . . be not wise in thy own conceit." (*Prov.* 3:5, 7). And St. Jerome calls that pride intolerable by which we give others to understand that we are so wise we do not need their advice: "Pride is unbearable, but to account oneself nothing needs counsel."[6]

---

4. *"Nihil hominem longius ab humilitate facit quam præsumptio virtutis propriæ."* (Lib. 22, Mor., cap. 3).
5. *"Ero humilior ex eo quod mihi deest."* (in *Ps.* 38).
6. *"Intolerabilis est superbia, existimare se nullius egere consilio."* (Cap. 1, *Is.*).

132. It is necessary to be humble, not only in one's thoughts, but also in one's words, because the humble man says little, following the counsel of the Holy Ghost: "Speak not anything rashly . . . let thy words be few." (*Eccles.* 5:1). To talk much proceeds from pride, because we are persuaded that we know a great deal and we wish to impress our thoughts and opinions on the minds of others.

Are you careful in speaking not to say anything in your own praise, or anything that might cause you to be praised by others; not to appear learned, wise or spiritual, ostentatiously displaying your personal advantages or those that belong to your family? It is easy in these things for you to be dominated by pride, and holy Tobias warns us, saying: "Never suffer pride to reign in thy mind, or in thy words." (*Tob.* 4:14).

Do you sometimes set yourself up as an example, saying it would be well to do so and so, as you have done it yourself? If you have some gift of God, do you talk about it, as if to say: "Thanks be to God, I have not such and such a vice; thanks be to God, I have such and such a virtue?" Call to remembrance the advice given by the angel to Tobias, that it is good to keep hidden the secret gifts of God: "For it is good to hide the secret of a king." (*Tob.* 12:7).

It may be that sometimes you speak ill of yourself, in order that others may contradict it. This is the way of him of whom it is said, "There is one that humbleth himself wickedly," (*Ecclus.* 19:23), who pretends indeed to flee from praise, yet seeks it, to flee from honors and courts them. You must accustom yourself not to speak either ill or well of yourself, because it is easy for pride to inspire your words in either case.

133. When you hear yourself praised, what precautions do you take? Self-love is quick to mingle some grain of its own incense with that which it receives from others. I mean by this that through the corruption of our nature we are very ready to approve these praises as if they were truly and justly due to us and to flatter ourselves with vainglory, but all this comes from lack of humility. St. Augustine, speaking of this pleasure which we derive from being praised, addresses this prayer to God: "Lord, put this folly far from me,"[7] for he held it as a real madness to take pleasure in vanity and deceits; and when he heard others praise him, he pondered upon the knowledge he had of himself and upon the justice of God, saying in his own heart: "I know myself better than they know me, but God knows me better than I know myself."[8]

A heart that is truly humble, says St. Gregory, always fears to hear its own praises, because it fears that this praise may either be false or may rob it of the merit and reward promised to true virtue. "If the heart is truly humble, the good that

---

7. *"Insaniam istam, Domine, longe fac a me."* (Lib. 10, *Confess.*, cap. 37).

8. *"Melius me ego novi quam ille; sed melius Deus quam ego."* (*Enarr. in Ps.* 25).

it hears of itself it either fails to recognize or fears lest the hope of future title to reward be changed for some passing favor."[9]

The humble man, says St. Thomas, is amazed when anyone speaks well of him, and there is nothing that astonishes him more than to hear himself praised. Thus, the Blessed Virgin, when she heard from the Archangel Gabriel that she was to become the Mother of God, had such a lowly opinion of herself that she marvelled greatly that she should be exalted to such an eminent dignity. "To a humble soul nothing is more wonderful than to hear its own excellence; thus, to Mary's saying, 'How shall this be?' the angel brings forward a proof, not to take away her belief, but rather to dispel her wonder."[10]

But pride may even insinuate itself into this very contempt of praise, as St. Augustine says: "A man is often foolishly proud of his own foolish contempt of himself."[11]

But if it be necessary for us to praise those who are present, it is not less necessary to exercise

---

9. *"Si cor veraciter humile est, bona, quæ de se audit, aut minime recognoscit aut pavet ne spes futuri muneris in mercedem permutetur transitorii favoris."* (*Lib.* 22, *Moral.* c. 3).

10. *"Animæ humili nihil est mirabilius quam auditus suæ excellentiæ. Sic Mariæ respondenti: Quomodo fiet istud? Angelus probationem inducit, non ad auferendam infidelitatem, sed magis ad removendam admirationem."* (*S.T.,* IIIa, Q. 30, art. 4).

11. *"Sæpe homo de ipso vano contemptu vanius gloriatur."* (*Lib.* 10).

discretion and prudence in so doing, as St. Augustine also teaches: "Lest the most dangerous temptation be found in the love of giving praise." [12]

Adulation is always pernicious, whether we adulate ourselves or others.

134. One can also sin against humility by the pomp and vanity of one's attire. This is what Queen Esther calls "the sign of my pride and glory," (*Esther* 14:16), and we must keep our hearts detached from such love because such attire is only right when it is suited to our state and condition, and when we wear it with the right intention: "Glory not in apparel at any time," (*Ecclus.* 11:4), says the Holy Ghost.

However beautiful the apparel that you wear may be, do not allow vainglory to enter your heart; and if you have to appear in public in state, guard yourself against vanity, "and be not exalted in the day of thy honor." (*Ecclus.* 11:4).

Excess, self-complacency, the desire to please, to attract attention to oneself, to be above one's equals, or to equal one's superiors by the gorgeousness of one's attire, are things to be moderated and subdued by humility. St. Thomas gives an excellent rule for this: "Extravagance in sumptuous apparel is to be restrained by humility." [13]

These necessities which we deem essential for

_____
12. *"Ne tentatio periculosissima in amore laudis immitatur."*
13. *"Superabundantia in exterioribus sumptibus per humilitatem est reprimenda."* (*S.T.,* IIa IIæ, Q. 161, art. 2).

the decorum of our state must have their limits prescribed by Christian modesty and simplicity, and not by pride or the luxurious tendency of the times. And the vanity with which our grace of bearing or beauty of face inspires us must also be restrained by humility, because "favor is deceitful and beauty is vain." (*Prov.* 31:30).

135. As to certain exterior actions, indifferent in themselves, but which if done with a good intention can tend to make us virtuous, the one necessary thing is to have a care that they be performed with humility, as Christ teaches us: "I will be little in my own eyes." (*2 Kgs.* 6:22). This is what each of us should say to himself, with holy King David, and it helps us greatly to form this good habit of humility toward ourselves, in order that we may also be humble to others.

This is why I wish you to apply yourself with all diligence to this examen. What conception and esteem have you of the virtue of humility? Do you really believe that humility of heart is necessary for your eternal salvation? You know that it is necessary to believe firmly in the mystery of the Holy Trinity and that whoever doubts it is a heretic, but you must know that it is also necessary to believe with equal firmness the doctrine of humility taught by Jesus Christ in His Gospel, because we cannot affirm that in the Gospel one doctrine is more true than another, nor that one must believe one more than another, because they all proceed equally from the mouth of Jesus

Christ, who is the very Truth.

If, therefore, you believe in this dogma of humility, how do you apply it to yourself, and what measures do you take in order to be humble? Do you ask it of God? Do you have recourse to the intercession of the Blessed Virgin and of the Saints? Do you make yourself familiar with those thoughts which are most efficacious to teach you this humility—the thoughts of death, judgment, Hell, Paradise and eternity, the grievousness of sin, and above all, the Passion of Jesus Christ?

I am perfectly certain that you will never attain to this humility if you neglect these means, which are the most appropriate by which to acquire it; and if you have not been humble of heart, how can you ever justify yourself before the tribunal of God?

Impress upon your mind this beautiful passage which St. Augustine left to his friend Dioscurus: "Do not depart, O Dioscurus, from the royal way of humility, which was taught by Christ; although many other virtues are commanded by the Christian religion, study to give humility the highest place, because all virtues are acquired and maintained by humility, and without humility they vanish away." [14]

---

14. *"Jesu Christi, oro te, mi Dioscure, ut tota pietate subdas velim, nec aliam tibi ad capessendam veritatem viam munias quam quæ ab illo munita est: ea est autem humilitas."* (*Epist.* 113).

∽6∾

Moral Doctrine

On the Vice of Pride and the Best Use to be Made of the Practical Examen

S T. Thomas defines pride as an inordinate affection against right reason, by which man esteems himself and desires to be esteemed by others above that which he really is.[1] And as this affection is opposed to right reasoning, it is certainly a sin which partakes of the gravity of a mortal sin, because it is in direct opposition to the virtue of humility. And St. Paul puts the proud in the same category as those whom "God delivered . . . up to a reprobate sense . . ." and "are worthy of death," (*Rom.* 1:28, 32), although sometimes it is only a venial sin, when the reason is not sufficiently enlightened, or there is not full consent of the will.[2]

137. Pride is placed among the deadly sins, because it is from pride that so many other sins are derived, and that is why St. Paul, seeing the innumerable wickedness of the world, called them

---

1. *S.T.,* IIa IIæ, Q. 162, art. 1.
2. D. Th., loc. cit., art. 5.

to the notice of his disciple Timothy, saying: "Look how many are haughty, proud, blasphemers, disobedient to parents," (*Tim.* 3:2), without love for their neighbor or for God. From whence do you suppose all these vices derive their origin? This is the source: the inordinate love which everyone has for himself. "Men are lovers of themselves." This is the explanation which St. Paul gives to it, and as St. Augustine observes, "All these evils flow from the source which he first mentions—self-love,"[3] and as the same Saint says, "This excess of self-love is only pride."

Therefore, we can conclude from this that whoever overcomes pride overcomes a whole host of sins, according to the explanation given by St. Gregory[4] of this text of Job: "He smelleth the battle afar off, and the shouting of the army." (*Job* 39:25).

138. Pride holds the first place among the deadly sins, and St. Thomas not only places it among the deadly sins, but above them, as transcending them all, the king of vices, which includes in his *cortège* all the other vices. Therefore, it is called in Holy Scripture: "The root of all evil," (*1 Tim.* 6:10), "The beginning of all sin," (*Ecclus.* 10:15), because as the root of the tree is hidden under the earth and sends all its strength up into the branches, so

---

3. *"Hæc omnia mala ab eo veluti fonte manant, quod primum posuit seipsos amantes."* (Tr. 123 *in Jo. lib.* 4, *De Civ. Dei*, c. 13).
4. *Lib.* 31, *Mor.* c. 17.

pride remains hidden in the heart and secretly influences every sin through its action. Therefore, whenever we commit a mortal sin, we are in reality opposing and directing our own will against the Will of God.

Job speaks thus of the sinner: "He hath strengthened himself against the Almighty," (*Job* 15:25), and in this sense one can also say of pride that it is the greatest of all sins, because the proud rebel against God, setting themselves in opposition to God; nor do they mind displeasing God in order to please themselves, leaving the All to attach themselves to their own nothingness, as St. Augustine says: "Abandoning God, he seeks his own will, and by so doing, draws near to nothingness; hence the proud, according to Scripture, are called doers of their own will,"[5] which is to say with St. Paul: "Lovers of themselves." (*2 Tim.* 3:2). And the same holy Father[6] makes this reflection, that even venial sins committed more from frailty than from malice may become mortal if they are aggravated by pride. "Sins creep in through human weakness, and although small, they become great and heavy if pride adds to their weight and measure."[7]

But since God has sworn to detest this vice,

---

5. *"Relicto Deo, quærit sibi placere et nihilo propinquare."* (Lib. 4, *De Civ. Dei,* C. 14).

6.-7. *"Subrepunt ex humana fragilitate peccata; et quamvis parva eadem ipsa fiunt magna et gravia, si eis superbia incrementum et pondus adjecerit."* (*Lib. de Sancta Virginit.* C. 2).

"The Lord God hath sworn by his own soul, I detest the pride of Jacob," (*Amos* 6:8), what wonder is it that He should punish it more than all vices? St. Augustine remarks with singular force that among all the sins by which sinners fall, none is so great, so ruinous, or so grave as that of pride. "Among all the falls of sinners, none is so great as that of the proud."[8]

139. Let us now consider wherein lies the terrible danger of this vice: 1) Because while all other vices destroy only their opposite virtues, as wantonness destroys chastity, greediness temperance, and anger gentleness, etc., pride destroys all virtue and is, according to St. Gregory, like a cancer which not only eats away one limb, but attacks the whole body: "Like a widespread pestilential disease."[9]

2) Because the other vices are to be feared only when we are disposed to evil; but pride, says St. Augustine, insinuates itself even when we are trying to do good. "Other vices are to be feared in sins; pride is to be feared even in good deeds."[10] And St. Isidore says: "Pride is worse than every other vice from the fact that it springs even from virtue and its guilt is less felt."[11]

3) Because after having fought against and over-

---

8. *"Inter omnes homines peccantium lapsus nulla est gravior quam superborum ruina."* (*Ps.* 35).
9. *"Quasi generalis ac pestifer morbus."* (*Lib.* 34, *Mor.,* C. 18).
10. *Cætera vitia in peccatis; superbia etiam in recte factis timenda est."* (*Epist.* 118).
11. *"Omni vitio superbia deterior est eo quod de opere virtutis exeritur minusve ejus culpa sentitur."* (*Lib. de Summ. Bono*).

come the other vices, we may justly rejoice; but as soon as we begin to rejoice that we have triumphed over pride, it triumphs over us and becomes victorious over us in that very act for which we are praising ourselves for conquering it. St. Augustine says: "When a man rejoices that he has overcome pride, he lifts up his head for very joy and says: "Behold, I triumph thus because thou dost triumph."[12]

4) Because if the other vices are of quick growth, we can also rid ourselves of them quickly; but pride is the first vice we learn, and it is also the last to leave us, as St. Augustine says: "For those who are returning to God, pride is the last thing to be overcome, as it was the first cause of their leaving God."[13]

5) Because as we have need of some special grace of God in order to enable us to do any of those good works that pertain to our eternal salvation, so there is no vice which prevents the influx of grace so much as pride, because "God resists the proud." (*James* 4:6).

6) Because pride is the characteristic and most significant sign of the reprobate, as St. Gregory says: "Pride is the most manifest sign of the lost."[14]

7) Because the other vices are easily recogniz-

---

12. *"Ubi lætatus fuerit homo se superasse superbiam ex ipsa lætitia caput erigit et dicit: Ecce ego ideo triumpho, quia triumphas."* (Aug., *Lib. de Nat. et Gr.* C. 27).
13. *"Hoc est ultimum redeuntibus ad Deum quod recedentibus primum fuit."* (*Enarr.* 2 in *Ps.* 118).
14. *"Evidentissimum reproborum signum superbia est."* (*Lib.* 34, *Mor.* 118).

able, and therefore it is easy to hate them and to amend; but pride is a vice that is not so easily known because it goes masked and disguised in many forms, even putting on the semblance of virtue and the very appearance of humility; thus being a hidden vice, it is less easy to escape from it, as is taught in the maxim of St. Ambrose: "Hidden things are more difficult to avoid than things known."[15]

140. This last danger is for us the greatest of all, and all the more because we ourselves seem to cooperate, in order not to recognize this vice, inventing titles, colors, artifices to conceal its ugliness, and studying innumerable pretexts in order to deceive ourselves into believing that pride is not pride and does not reign in our heart at the very moment when it is more dominant than ever.

As humility is generally called weak and contemptible by the blind lovers of this world, so pride is called courage and greatness, and the proud are said to be spirited, dignified, of noble behavior and good judgment, sustaining their position with honor, maintaining their reputation, keeping up their rank and fulfilling the duties of their state. What a vocabulary of vanity! But let us set against it the vocabulary of truth which was used by Job: "I have said to rottenness: Thou art my father; to worms, my mother and my sister." (*Job* 17:14).

---

15. *"Difficilius caventur occulta quam cognita."* (*Epist.* 82).

If you sift through these worldly expressions, you will find that the quintessence of a most consummate pride issues therefrom. This is indeed the only thing I ask of you, that if you have unfortunately been deceived by others, you will at least not deceive yourselves. Study to know your own ills, if you wish to be cured of them. I recommend you only to apply yourselves to learn the truth and profit by this advice, that if the knowledge of this truth seems difficult to you, it is a sign that you are proud.

It is St. Thomas himself who will convince you of this. You can learn truth in two ways, that is, by the intellect and by the affections. The proud man does not know it by his intellect, because God hides it from him, as Christ said: "Thou hast hid these things from the wise and prudent." (*Matt.* 11:25). "And still less will he know it with his affection, because no one who takes pleasure in vanity can take pleasure in truth. "When the proud delight in their own excellence," explains St. Augustine, "they recede from the excellence of truth."[16]

The proud man does not take any pleasure in sermons, meditations, instructions concerning eternal truth; in fact, they are wearisome to him. If you discover any signs of this in yourself, you must at once conclude that you are proud, and humble yourself a little, O You who read this doc-

---

16. *"Superbi dum delectantur in propria, excellentia veritatis fastidiunt."* (D. Th. IIa IIae, Q. 162, art. 3).

trine, in order that the eternal Father of all light may give you light, even as Christ said: "I confess to Thee, O Father . . . thou hast revealed them to little ones." (*Matt.* 11:25).

141. St. Gregory and St. Thomas teach that one can sin in four different ways by one's own acts of pride. The *first* is when we hold that we have any good, either bodily or spiritual, of ourselves and glory in it as really belonging to us, without thinking of God, who is the giver of all good gifts. It is with this pride that Arfaxad, King of the Medes, sinned when he gloried in the power of his enormous army; and King Nabuchodonosor sinned likewise when he boasted of the building of Babylon: "Is not this the great Babylon, which I have built . . . by the strength of my power?" (*Dan.* 4:27). In the same way the rich man, mentioned in St. Luke, sinned when he took such pleasure in his riches and regarded them as his own substance, saying: "I will gather all things . . . and will say to my soul: Soul, thou hast much goods laid up for many years." (*Luke* 12:18, 19). And, therefore, we may say that it is through this pride that all sin who flatter themselves and are ostentatious, glorifying themselves, either for their great talents, or for their riches, or their prudence, or their eloquence, or the beauty of their body, or the costliness of their apparel, as if God had nothing to do with it, and who, esteeming themselves immoderately, desire also to be esteemed by others.

This is true pride, because if God had given all these good things for our use, He has reserved the glory of them for Himself. "To . . . the only God be honor and glory," (*1 Tim.* 1:17), and whoever usurps this glory is guilty of pride.

And therefore we must observe with St. Thomas that, in order to commit a sin of pride, it is not necessary to declare positively that these gifts do not come from God, for this would be a sin of infidelity, but it is enough that we should glory in them, as if they belonged to us, "which relates to pride."[17]

142. The *second* way in which we can sin in our actions by pride is when, knowing and admitting that we have received such and such a gift of God, we nevertheless attribute it inwardly to our own merit and desire that others should do so likewise, and in our exterior demeanor we behave as if we had indeed deserved to receive these gifts. It was thus that Lucifer sinned through pride; for being infatuated with his own beauty and nobility, and although he recognized that God was the author of it all, he nevertheless had the presumption to think that he had merited it himself and was worthy to sit beside God in the highest Heaven: "I will ascend into heaven." (*Is.* 14:13).

And, therefore, St. Bernard reproves him, saying: "O proud Soul, what work hast thou done that

---

17. *"Quod pertinet ad superbiam."* (IIa IIæ, Q. 162).

thou shouldst take thy rest?"[18] What hast thou
done, O Bold One, to deserve such an honor? And
it is thus that those reprobates sinned through
pride to whom allusion is made in *Luke* 17:9, who,
like the Pharisee, gave thanks to God for the good
they did and the evil they left undone: "O God, I
give Thee thanks . . ." etc.; but yet, at the same
time, they had the presumption to consider themselves of singular merit, "trusting in themselves."

Thus all those who sin by presuming that they
have deserved any good whatsoever of God are
convicted of pride, because by attesting to their
own merit, they make God a debtor of this grace,
which would no longer be grace if we had
deserved it. We may well be permitted, with Job,
to say that by our sins we have deserved God's
anger and every kind of evil: "Oh, that my sins,
whereby I have deserved wrath . . . were weighed
in a balance," (*Job* 6:2), but we cannot say that we
deserve grace or any good, as St. Paul says: "If by
grace, it is not now by works: otherwise, grace is
no more grace." (*Rom.* 11:6).

And each one of us should say with the same
humble St. Paul, "By the grace of God, I am what
I am." (*1 Cor.* 15:10). If I am rich, noble, sane or
possess any other gifts, it all comes from God, who
has made me thus; not because of my own merits,
but solely through His own mercy and goodness.
Whether I abstain from evil or whether I do good,
I owe it all, not to my own merit, but to the grace

18. *"O impudens, quid laborasti ut jam sedeas?"*

of God, who assists me with His mercy; "By the grace of God, I am what I am." (*1 Cor.* 15:10). And anyone who ascribes what he is or what he has to his own merits is guilty of pride and appropriates to himself what he ought to give to the mercy and grace of God. Therefore, Holy Church wisely ends her prayers with these words: "Through Jesus Christ our Lord . . ." etc. And by this we protest to the divine Majesty that we ask the gifts mentioned in those prayers through the merits of Jesus Christ and that, if our prayers are heard, it will only be through the merits of Jesus Christ.

This is a point which is worthy of all attention so that we may not fall, through inadvertence, into most terrible pride. And St. Augustine urges us to remember that, not only all the good we have comes from God, but also that we have it only through His mercy and not through our own merits. "When a man sees that whatever good he has is from the mercy of God, and not from his own merits, he ceases to be proud."[19]

143. The *third* way in which we can sin through pride is when we attribute to ourselves some good (of any kind whatsoever) which we do not really possess, but whether it be that we esteem ourselves for that imaginary good, which exists only in our thoughts, and desire others to esteem us for

---

19. *"Cum viderit homo quia quidquid boni habet de Dei misericordia est, non de meritis ipsius, non superbit."* (In *Ps.* 84).

it also, or whether we really possess it, or whether again, we only desire to have this good which we have not, in order to be able to boast of it and glory in it—all this is detestable pride.

It was in this way that the Bishop of Laodicea sinned by esteeming himself rich in merit, when he was merely contemptible; and therefore God told him that he would vomit him out of His mouth. "I will begin to vomit thee out of My mouth, because thou sayest, I am rich . . . and have need of nothing, and knowest not that thou art . . . miserable and poor." (*Apoc.* 3:16-17). And it is with this kind of pride that all sin who either esteem themselves or who seek to be esteemed by others, in word or deed, for more riches, knowledge, rank or virtue than they really have.

It may be an act of virtue to desire these things for some honorable end, for instance to desire more knowledge in order to be able to serve Holy Church, to desire riches in order to be able to give more alms. But to desire these things in order not to seem inferior to others, or to acquire more esteem, is only pride, and oh, how few there are who are not infected with this pride! One for one thing, and one for another, almost all men seek to be esteemed above what they really are—and this without the slightest scruple.

Sometimes it may be that the sin is not so grave, either because this is not a deliberate wish, or else because the nature of the offense is very slight; but on the other hand, it is in itself always a very grave sin, because through this pride, man no longer remains subject to that rule which has been given him by God—to be contented in his own state. St. Thomas says: "This is evidently of the nature of mortal sin,"[20] and his doctrine on this point is that the greater the gift may be in which we glory, although we do not possess it, the greater is our pride. Therefore, it is worse to affect to be holy than to affect to be noble or rich, because sanctity is a greater gift than rank or wealth. And the habit of excusing the sins we have committed also belongs to this kind of pride, because when we excuse ourselves and say that we are not guilty, we assert our innocence and accredit ourselves with an innocence which we do not possess. And how often do we sin thus through pride, without even knowing it!

And St. Thomas also attributes to pride the endeavor to conceal our sins and so excuse and palliate the wickedness thereof in our Confessions. (*Ibid.* art. 4).

144. The *fourth* way in which we sin through pride is when we use any gift we may possess in order to appear distinguished or to think ourselves better than others, and to be more esteemed and honored than they. Whatever good we have, whether of body or soul, of nature, fortune or grace, is a gift of God, and to use these gifts in order to try to be more conspicuous

---

20. *"Et hoc manifestum est quod habet rationem peccati mortalis."* (IIa IIæ, Q. 162, art. 5 et 6).

than others is pride.

It is with this pride that the Pharisee in the Temple regarded his own goodness and placed himself above others, especially the Publican. "I am not as the rest of men, extortioners, unjust, adulterers, as also is this publican." (*Luke* 18:11). He esteemed himself above all, and was in reality the proudest of all. It was with this pride, too, that the disciples sinned when they gloried in their singular gift of being able to cast out devils: "And they returned with joy, saying: 'Lord, the devils also are subject to us.'" (*Luke* 10:17). And Our Blessed Lord answered them most justly: "I saw Satan like lightning falling from heaven," (*Luke* 10:18), as if He almost meant to say, "Take care that you do not exalt yourself like the proud Lucifer, lest you fall as he did."

St. Gregory in fact makes this reflection, that there is no pride which resembles the diabolical pride so much as this: "This comes very near to a diabolical likeness."[21] Whoever wishes to exalt himself above others imitates Lucifer, who desired to be first among the Angels and nearest to the throne of God. This was the sin of Lucifer when he dwelt upon his desire to be exalted: "And thou saidst in thy heart, I will ascend." (*Is.* 14:13). And those who are always scheming for their own advancement and are discontented with their own state, sin even as Lucifer sinned: "I will

---

21. *"Hæc similitudini diabolicæ vicinius appropinquat."* (Lib. 23, *Mor.* cap. 4).

ascend." (*Is.* 14:13). And we ought to guard against this diabolical sin, as St. Paul says: "Lest being puffed up with pride, he fall into the judgment of the devil." (*1 Tim.* 3:6).

And, moreover, we ought also to observe what the same holy Pontiff tells us, that we often fall into this the worst kind of pride: "Into this fourth kind of pride the human mind falls very frequently."[22] And there is no doubt that it is really a grievous sin, for we thereby offend both God and our neighbor. And how many men and women there are, both religious and secular, of every state and condition, who commit this sin of pride so frequently that it becomes a predominant habit with them.

Practically, we notice that all men desire to be distinguished in their own particular art, however inferior it may be, and all seek first to be esteemed as much as others, and then to be distinguished more than others—"I will ascend," (*Is.* 14:13)—each one in his own sphere and also outside his own sphere. The rich man regards himself as greater than the learned man on account of his riches; the learned man as greater than the rich man on account of his learning; the chaste man esteems himself better than the one who gives alms, and the one who gives alms esteems himself more highly than the man who is chaste. Oh, what pride! And yet few people are willing to

---

22. *"In hac arrogantiæ quarta specie crebro humanus animus labitur."*

recognize that they are proud.

145. The holy Pope St. Gregory discerns pride in all kinds of people and describes its characteristics. Some, he says, are proud of their possessions, others of their eloquence, some are proud of mundane things and some of things of the Church and the gifts of God. Although blinded by vanity, we are unable to discern it, and whether we exalt ourselves above others on account of worldly glory or of spiritual gifts, pride has never left our heart, because it is domiciled there, and to disguise itself, assumes a false appearance.

It is also well to know that pride does not tempt superiors and inferiors in the same way. It tempts the great by giving them to understand that they have attained to their position by their own merit and that none of their inferiors could be compared to them. It tempts their subordinates by diverting their attention from their own faults and making them observe and judge the doings of their superiors. They speak nevertheless of and to their superiors with a certain liberty, and as this pride is called a rightful independence in them, so in the superior it is called zeal and decorum.

Sometimes our pride constrains us to talk loud, at other times to preserve a bitter silence. Pride is dissolute in its joys, somber and raving in its melancholy. It seems honorable in appearance, yet is without honor; it is full of valor in giving offense, but cowardly in taking it; it is slow to obey, importunate in its demands to ascertain its duty, but negligent in performing it. While it is prompt to meddle and interfere in all that does not concern it, there is no possibility of bending it in any direction unless it is inclined thereto by its own taste. And it is astute and pretends to be indifferent about having any office or dignity which it covets, so that it may be forced into accepting them, loving to have those things which it most desires thrust violently upon it, for fear it should be regarded with contempt if its desire for them were made known. This is all St. Gregory's teaching.

146. After considering pride in itself, it remains for us to observe its effects, and especially eight of the more common and familiar vices which it produces—which are *presumption, ambition, envy, vainglory, boastfulness, hypocrisy, disobedience* and *discord*. Let us examine them with St. Thomas.

Presumption is a vice by which we esteem ourselves able to achieve things beyond our strength, forgetful of the necessity of divine help. The sinner is guilty of presumption when he believes that he can be converted to God whenever he likes and chooses—as if conversion were the work of his own free-will alone—and living ill, yet trusts to make a good death; when he sins and goes on sinning, relying upon obtaining ultimate forgiveness; when he believes that he can of himself and without the help of grace, both withstand temptation, avoid sin and observe the commandments of God, or else that he can make some supernatural act of faith, hope, charity or contrition, or perform some meritorious act toward his eternal welfare, and save himself by persevering in well-doing.

All this is beyond our own strength, and to think that we can do these things without the special help of God and without being willing to ask this help of God is a sin of presumption—a grave sin of that pride by which we believe that we possess a virtue when we have it not. "O wicked presumption," says Holy Writ, "whence camest thou?" (*Ecclus.* 37:3). And St. Gregory, explaining what that sin was which Job called "great iniquity," (*Job* 31:28), affirmed that it was presumption, which is an insult to the Author of all grace, "by which a man takes all the credit of a good work to himself."[23]

147. *Ambition* is a vice which makes us seek our own honor with inordinate avidity.[24] Now, as this honor is a mark of respect and esteem, given for meritorious virtue and to him who is of superior degree, and as it is certain that we have no merit of ourselves, because everything we receive comes from God, it is not to ourselves, but to God alone that such honor is wholly due.

Moreover, as this honor has been ordained by God as a means to render us capable of helping our neighbor, it is certain that all such honor must be

---

23. *"Qua sibi vires boni operis arrogat."* (*Lib.* 22, *Mor.,* cap. 10).
24. *S.T.,* IIa IIæ, Q. 131, art. 2.

used by us in fulfillment of this end. Two things therefore are needful to enable us to flee from ambition. The first is that we should not appropriate merit of the honor, and the second is that we should confess that this same honor is due wholly to God and is only dear to us in so far as it can serve our neighbor. If therefore we are wanting in one of these two things, we commit the sin of ambition.

He is ambitious, therefore, who seeks to have some office or position, whether in the world or in the Church, when he has not the requisite virtue and knowledge to maintain it, and who schemes and plots to be put before others who are more worthy than he.

He is ambitious who desires to be esteemed, honored and revered more than his position merits, and as if he were of higher rank than he is: to be honored as an eloquent preacher or as a clever writer, or in any profession to which he may belong, although in reality he can only be classed among the indifferent and mediocre.

He is ambitious who, without a single thought for the glory of God, or of serving his neighbor, desires or seeks some worldly or ecclesiastical office, simply with a view to his own temporal welfare and for the advancement of his family, or who wishes to gain the honor of some high office or bishopric, "from the love of power," as St. Augustine says, "and from pride of place."[25]

---

25. *"Dominandi cupiditate et principandi superbia."* (*Lib.* 19, *De Civ. Dei.*, cap. 14).

Jesus Christ shows a special hatred for this vice in several places in His Gospel (*Matt.* 18:20, 23; *Luke* 9:12), and the Fathers argue from this that the ambitious man is in a state of mortal sin, and it is easy for the most spiritual persons to commit this sin. As St. Ambrose says, "Ambition often makes criminals of those whom no vice would delight, whom no lust could move, whom no avarice could deceive."[26]

The worst of ambition is that few people have any scruples about it, and the reason is that by this vice conscience is depraved, because it is united to this passion and seldom recovers its integrity.[27]

148. *Envy* is a sadness arising from the contemplation of our neighbor's welfare, when we imagine that the good which happens to him must be to our own detriment, prejudicial to our own glory and interest. But of his goods, we only envy those which bring us esteem in the eyes of the world—riches, dignity, the friendship and favors of the great, science, praise, fame and all that which seems to us to contribute to our credit and to bring us honor.

And it is thus that envy is born within us, when we see one who is richer, more learned than we are, another wiser and more virtuous than we,

---

26. "*Sæpe quos vitia nulla delectant, quos nulla potuit movere luxuria, nulla avaritia subvertere, facit ambitio criminosos.*" (*Lib.* 4 *in Luc.*).
27. *S.T.,* IIa IIæ, Q. 131, art. 1 et 2; Q. 185, art. 2.

another who has more talent and ability and whom therefore we should like to see deprived of these gifts in order that he might also be deprived of the praise and honor and any other advantages which we imagine are more due to us than to him.

Now the sin consists in this, that when we ought, from a sense of charity, to rejoice at our neighbor's prosperity, we are only saddened at it, wishing in our pride that it might be ours, in order that we might be superior to our neighbor in merit. And this sin is the especial sin of the devil, as the Wise Man says, "the envy of the devil." (*Wis.* 2:24). And therefore the Holy Ghost most justly commands us through St. Paul to guard against it: "Let us not be . . . envying one another," (*Gal.* 5:26), as it is easy to sin mortally in one way or another. But nevertheless, how common this vice is in families, in communities, in every state of life, to high and low, rich and poor, to seculars, and even to the Religious themselves!

All this evil proceeds from a false conscience, which leads us to believe that envy is not a great sin, and therefore, although it be a grievous evil, it is neither feared, nor avoided, nor do we study to amend ourselves of it. This reflection is from St. Cyprian: "Envy seems a small offense, so that, while it seems slight to us, it is not feared; while it is not feared, it is despised; while it is despised, it is not easily avoided, and thus [it] becomes a secret source of ruin."[28]

---

28. *"Invidia leve crimen videtur: dumque existimatur leve*

149. *Vainglory* consists in an inordinate appetite for praise and a desire that our merit should shine forth with glory, and in three different ways this glory can be called vain and wicked:

Firstly, when we seek to be praised for a virtue or any other gift of body or soul which we do not possess, or else to be praised for some frail transitory possession which is not worthy of praise, such as health, beauty and other gifts of the body, riches, pomp and other goods which are called the gifts of fortune.

Secondly, when in seeking praise we value the esteem and approbation of one whose judgment is unreliable.

Thirdly, when we do not use this praise either for the honor of God or the good of our neighbor, and this is always to sin against the dictates of Holy Scripture: "Let nothing be done through contention, neither by vain glory . . ." (*Phil.* 2:3). And it can be a mortal sin when we seek to be praised for some wrong which we have done or have the intention of doing, or for some other wrong which we have never done and have had no thought of doing; or else to accept praise for a good which we have not done and which we want to make others believe that we have done. It can also be a mortal sin if we do good only out of human respect, with the intention of being seen and praised.

---

esse, non timetur; dum non timetur, contemnitur; dum contemnitur, non facile vitatur; et fit cæca et occulta pernicies." See also St. Thomas, IIa IIæ, Q. 34, art. 6; et Q. 16, art. 1 et 2, etc.; et Q. 158, art. 11 et 14.

In short, this is always a very dangerous sin, not so much because of its gravity, as on account of its grave consequence and because it prevents the soul from receiving the help of grace and disposes it to various mortal sins: "Vainglory is said to be a dangerous sin, not so much on account of its gravity, as because it is a disposition to grievous sins, in so far as it gradually disposes a man to the loss of all inner good."[29]

He who suffers from vainglory is also in danger of losing his faith, according to the saying of Christ: "How can you believe, who receive glory one from another?" (*John* 5:44). St. Augustine, reflecting upon this and how little this great evil is known, affirms that none is wiser than he who knows that this love of praise is a vice: "He sees best who sees that love of praise is a vice."[30]

150. *Boastfulness* is a vice by which man, desiring to be supremely honored above all others, begins to praise and exalt himself, exaggerating and amplifying things, in order to make his own merit appear greater than it is. It is also called ostentation, self-praise or frowardness [i.e., will-

---

29. "*Inanis gloria dicitur esse periculosum peccatum non tantum propter gravitatem, sed etiam propter hoc, quod est dispositio ad gravia peccata, in quantum scilicet paullatim disponit ad hoc quod homo privetur interioribus bonis.*" (D. Th. IIa IIæ, Q. 132, art. 3).
30. "*Sanius videt qui amorem laudis vitium esse cognoscit.*" (*Lib.* 5, *De Civ. Dei*, cap. 13. See also *S.T.*, IIa IIæ, Q. 21, art. 4; et Q. 305, art. 1; et Q. 131, per tot.; et Q. 178, art. 2).

ful contrariness], and St. Augustine calls it, "The worst of all pests,"[31] and St. Ambrose calls it a net spread by the devil to catch the strongest and most spiritual: "The devil lays snares such as entrap the strongest."[32] And this is a vice which is beyond measure, because in vaunting ourselves for that which we have not, we lie to our own conscience and to God; and as God said of Moab by the prophet: "He is exceeding proud . . . I know his boasting, and that the strength thereof is not according to it." (*Jer.* 48:29-30).

It can be a mortal sin when we boast of some sin which we have committed; when we praise ourselves, despising others; or else when we praise and exalt ourselves through an excess of pride, which abounds in the heart.

The Angelic Doctor notes that this is an ordinary and not an infrequent case and that the habit is easily formed.[33]

151. *Hypocrisy* is a vice by which we affect to demonstrate externally a virtue and a sanctity which we do not possess; and he is really a hypocrite who, being full of wickedness within, pretends in his outward appearance to be good.

There is no vice against which Jesus Christ has

---

31. *"Nocentiorem omnibus pestem."* (Lib. 1 *De Ord.* cap. 11).
32. *"Diabolus jactantiam prætendit, quæ etiam fortes decipit."* (*Lib. in Luc.*)
33. *S.T.,* IIa IIæ, Q. 112, art. 1. See also *S.T.,* IIa IIæ, Q. 110, art. 2; Q. 112, art. 1; et Q. 132, art. 5 ad 1; et Q. 162, art. 4 ad 2.

inveighed so much in His Gospel as against this one (*Matt.* 23:13, 14, 15, 23, 25, 27, 28, 29), condemning it with eight cries of "Woe to you," which are eight maledictions. And St. Gregory remarks that the hypocrites, blinded by pride and hardened in their sins, generally die impenitent, without ever being enlightened, for a reason which is perhaps taken from St. Peter Chrysologus, because while we can see that the remedies to the amendment of other vices do good, the disease of hypocrisy is so pestilential that it affects the very remedies themselves, so that they only serve to foment and increase the evil. "Brethren," says the Saint, "this pestilence must be avoided that turns remedies into diseases, medicines into maladies, holiness into vice, saintliness into sinfulness."[34]

Hypocrisy is always a mortal sin when we pretend to be spiritual and holy, and try to appear as such when we are not so at heart, caring more for the opinion of men than for the opinion of God. And it is worse still when we affect sanctity in order to further our own advancement and to acquire credit in order to reach and to work evil, or else to obtain some honor or other temporal good.

In this way also we sin gravely by hypocrisy when we show ourselves scrupulous about works of supererogation [things beyond what duty requires] or in certain minute observances, not fearing at the same time to transgress against the

---

34. *"Fratres, hæc pestilentia fugienda est quæ de remediis creat morbos, conficit de medicina languorem, sanctitatem vertit in crimen."*

essential duties of religion and our own state of life, "having left the weightier things of the law," like those Scribes and Pharisees whom Christ reproved, saying that they "strain a gnat and swallow a camel." (*Matt.* 23:24).

Also, when in all the functions connected with the service of God, we pretend to have a pure intention when we have it not: "And seek to please, not God but men, not the conversion, but the favor of the people."[35]

The Fathers generally call hypocrisy perversity, iniquity, impiety; and it is easy not only to fall into this sin, but to become so accustomed to it that it leads us into atheism. We often begin by serving God with a certain degree of holy fervor, but when this diminishes, we no longer serve God, but only pretend to serve Him, in order to keep up outward appearances. "Woe to you . . . hypocrites!"[36] (*Matt.* 23:13, ff.).

152. *Disobedience* is a sin by which we violate the command of our superiors, treating them with contempt; and it can be a mortal sin, even in small matters, because as St. Bernard says, we must not consider the nature of the thing commanded, nor the simple transgression of the precept, but the pride of the will which will not submit when it ought. "It is not the simple trans-

---

35. *"Et quærit non placere Deo, sed hominibus, non conversionem hominum sed auras favorum."* (D. Th. IIa IIæ, Q. 61, art. 2).
36. See *S.T.*, IIa IIæ, Q. 11 per tot.

gression of the wish, but the proud contention of the will that creates criminal disobedience,"[37] and the grievousness of the sin can be judged under three different heads.

First, the rank of the superior, because the higher the one who commands, the more grave is the disobedience. It is a greater sin to disobey God than to disobey man, a greater sin to disobey the Pope than a bishop, or a father and mother than other relations; and it is also a greater sin to disobey with contempt of the person who commands than with contempt only of the commandment.

Secondly, with respect to the nature of the things commanded, because when these are of greater importance, especially in the laws of God, the disobedience is greater. Therefore it is a graver sin to disobey those precepts which enjoin the love of God than those which command us to love our neighbor.

Thirdly, with respect to the form of the command by which the superior expresses his intention that he wishes to be obeyed in such and such a matter, but it is principally pride that aggravates the disobedience, as the will refuses to submit as it should to divine law.[38]

153. *Discord* is a discrepancy of the will which prevents it from conforming to the Will of God in

37. *"Non jussionis simplex ipsa transgressio, sed voluntatis superba contentio criminalem facit inobedientiam."* (*Lib. de Præcept et Dispens.*, cap. 11).
38. *S.T.*, IIa IIæ, Q. 69, art. 1; et Q. 105 per tot.

such matters as it ought to conform for the glory of God and the good of the neighbor; and it is a grave sin because St. Paul counts dissensions among those sins which exclude those who commit them from the kingdom of Heaven. (*Gal.* 5:20). And God declares His hatred and abhorrence of all those that disseminate discord among their neighbors. (*Prov.* 6:16, 19). Dissensions arise generally from pride, which prompts us to overesteem ourselves and to set our own welfare and opinions against those of others, and from this arises the quarreling, litigation, obstinacy, slandering, faction, hatred, strife and many other evils without number and without end.[39]

Recollect yourself now interiorly, and examine yourself, and having found that under one or other of these headings, pride really dominates you, judge how necessary it is for you to fight against it with humility, because if pride is conquered, a host of other sins will be conquered also. And in order to give yourself courage, remember this, that before the tribunal of God, the proud will be condemned and only the humble can hope to find mercy. To say that we are humble is the same as to say that we are among the elect and shall be saved; and to say that we are proud is the same as to say we are reprobate and lost. "Pride is a sure sign of the reprobate, as

---

39. *S.T.*, IIa IIæ, Q. 37, art. 1 et 2; et Q. 38, art. 2; et Q. 132, art. 5.

humility is the sign of the elect."[40] We owe this conclusion to St. Gregory.

Praised be Jesus Christ!

---

40. "*Evidentissimum reproborum signum est superbia; sicut e contra humilitas electorum.*" (*Hom.* 7 *in Evang.*; et *Lib.* 3, *Mor.* cap. 17).

CPSIA information can be obtained
at www.ICGtesting.com
Printed in the USA
LVHW030124090323
741211LV00033B/1427

9 781684 227983